SHARE the Music

MACMILLAN McGRAW-HILL

AUTHORS

Judy Bond,
   Coordinating Author
René Boyer-White
Margaret Campbelle-duGard
Marilyn Copeland Davidson,
   Coordinating Author
Robert de Frece
Mary Goetze,
   Coordinating Author
Doug Goodkin

Betsy M. Henderson
Michael Jothen
Carol King
Vincent P. Lawrence,
   Coordinating Author
Nancy L. T. Miller
Ivy Rawlins
Susan Snyder,
   Coordinating Author

Macmillan/McGraw-Hill School Publishing Company
New York • Columbus

Acknowledgments

Grateful acknowledgment is given to the following authors, composers, and publishers. Every effort has been made to trace the ownership of all copyrighted material and to secure the necessary permissions to reprint these selections. In the case of some selections for which acknowledgment is not given, extensive research has failed to locate the copyright holders.

Boosey & Hawkes, Inc. for *A New Year Carol*. Music by Benjamin Britten, Words Anonymous. © 1971 by Boosey & Hawkes Ltd. Reprinted by permission of Boosey & Hawkes, Inc. For *Dodi Li*, transcribed by Nira Chen. © Copyright 1992 by Boosey & Hawkes, Inc. Reprinted by permission. For *Fanfare for the Common Man* by Aaron Copland. © Copyright 1947 by Aaron Copland; Copyright Renewed. Used by permission of The Aaron Copland Fund for Music, Inc., Copyright Owner, and Boosey & Hawkes, Inc., Sole Licensee. For *Old Abram Brown*. Text by Walter de la Mare from TOM TIDDLER'S GROUND. Music by Benjamin Britten. © Copyright 1936 by Boosey & Co., Ltd.; Copyright Renewed. Reprinted by permission of Boosey & Hawkes, Inc. For *To Music* by Betty Bertaux. © 1987, 1989 by Boosey & Hawkes, Inc. Reprinted by permission. For *Wind on the Hill*. Music by Victoria Ebel-Sabo. © 1989 by Boosey & Hawkes, Inc. Reprinted by permission. *The Wind on the Hill* by A.A. Milne from NOW WE ARE SIX. © 1927 by E.P. Dutton & Co., Inc. Copyright renewal 1955 by A.A. Milne. Set to music by permission of the Trustees of the Pooh Properties.

Carnes D. Burson for *Go, My Son* by Arliene Nofchissey Williams and Carnes D. Burson, arrangement copyright © 1993, Carnes Burson. All rights reserved.

Wayne J. Chadwick for *A Is for Aesop* by Wayne J. Chadwick. © 1992 Wayne J. Chadwick. Reprinted by permission.

Cherry Lane Music Publishing Company, Inc. for *Feliz Navidad* by José Feliciano. © Copyright 1970 J & H Publishing Company. Administered by Cherry Lane Music Publishing Company, Inc. This Arrangement © Copyright 1994 J & H Publishing Company.

Frances Collin Literary Agency for *The Yesterdays and the Tomorrows* by Hal Borland. From SUNDIAL OF THE SEASONS. Reprinted by permission of Frances Collin, Literary Agent. Copyright © 1952, 1964 by Hal Borland. Copyright © renewed 1992 by Donal Borland.

CPP/Belwin, Inc. for *On the Trail* by Ferde Grofé. Copyright © 1931, 1932 (Renewed 1959, 1960) c/o EMI ROBBINS CATALOG INC. World Print Rights Controlled and Administered by CPP/Belwin, Inc., Miami, FL. All Rights Reserved. For *San Francisco*, music by Bronislaw Kaper and Walter Jurmann, lyrics by Gus Kahn. Copyright © 1936 (Renewed 1964) ROBBINS MUSIC CORPORATION. Rights Assigned to EMI CATALOGUE PARTNERSHIP. All Rights Controlled and Administered by EMI ROBBINS CATALOG, INC. All Rights Reserved. For *Shabat Shalom* by N. Frankel. Copyright © 1956 by Mills Music, Inc. International Copyright Secured. All Rights Reserved. For *Silver Bells* by R. Evans & J. Livingston. © 1950 by Paramount Music Corporation. Copyright Renewed 1977 by Paramount Music Corporation, 1 Gulf + Western Plaza, New York, NY 10023. International Copyright Secured. Made in USA. All Rights Reserved. For *The Theme from New York, New York* by Fred Ebb and John Kander. Copyright © 1977 UNITED ARTISTS CORPORATION. All Rights Controlled by UNART MUSIC CORPORATION. All Rights of UNART MUSIC CORPORATION Assigned to EMI CATALOGUE PARTNERSHIP. All Rights Administered by EMI UNART CATALOG INC. International Copyright Secured. Made in USA. All Rights Reserved. For *Tzena, Tzena*, folk song from Israel, words by Mitchell Parish, music by Issachar Miron and Julius Grossman. Copyright © 1950 by Mills Music Inc. Copyright Renewed. Used With Permission. All Rights Reserved.

Curtis Brown, Ltd. for *The Swallow* (in Teacher's Edition) by Ogden Nash from THE NEW NUTCRACKER SUITE AND OTHER INNOCENT VERSES. Copyright © 1962 by Ogden Nash. Reprinted by permission of Curtis Brown, Ltd.

Marilyn C. Davidson for *Gau Shan Ching*. English lyrics by Marilyn Davidson. Translation printed by permission. For *The Horseman*. Words by The Literary Trustees of Walter de la Mare and The Society of Authors as their representative. Music by permission of Marilyn C. Davidson © 1987.

Donaldson Publishing Co. for *Carolina in the Morning*, written by Walter Donaldson & Gus Kahn. Copyright © 1922, Renewed 1949 Donaldson Publishing Co. and Gilbert Keyes Music Co. All Rights Reserved. Used by Permission.

Doubleday for *Celebration* by Alonzo Lopez, from WHISPERING WIND by Terry Allen. Copyright © 1972 by the Institute of American Indian Arts. Used by permission of Doubleday, a division of Bantam Doubleday Dell Publishing Group, Inc.

continued on page 422

Macmillan/McGraw-Hill School Division
10 Union Square East
New York, New York 10003

Printed in the United States of America
ISBN 0-02-295054-0 / 5
3 4 5 6 7 8 9 VHJ 99 98 97 96 95

SPECIAL CONTRIBUTORS

Contributing Writer
Janet McMillion

Consultant Writers
Teri Burdette, Signing
Brian Burnett, Movement
Robert Duke, Assessment
Joan Gregoryk, Vocal Development/
  Choral
Judith Jellison, Special Learners/
  Assessment
Jacque Schrader, Movement
Kathy B. Sorensen, International Phonetic
  Alphabet
Mollie Tower, Listening

Consultants
Lisa DeLorenzo, Critical Thinking
Nancy Ferguson, Jazz/Improvisation
Judith Nayer, Poetry
Marta Sanchez, Dalcroze
Mollie Tower, Reviewer
Robyn Turner, Fine Arts

Multicultural Consultants
Judith Cook Tucker
JaFran Jones
Oscar Muñoz
Marta Sanchez
Edwin J. Schupman, Jr., of ORBIS
  Associates
Mary Shamrock
Kathy B. Sorensen

Multicultural Advisors
Shailaja Akkapeddi (Hindi), Edna Alba
(Ladino), Gregory Amobi (Ibu), Thomas
Appiah (Ga, Twi, Fanti), Deven Asay
(Russian), Vera Auman (Russian, Ukrainian),
David Azman (Hebrew), Lissa Bangeter
(Portuguese), Britt Marie Barnes (Swedish),
Dr. Mark Bell (French), Brad Ahawanrathe
Bonaparte (Mohawk), Chhanda Chakroborti
(Hindi), Ninthalangsonk Chanthasen
(Laotian), Julius Chavez (Navajo), Lin-Rong
Chen (Mandarin), Anna Cheng (Mandarin),
Rushen Chi (Mandarin), T. L. Chi (Mandarin),
Michelle Chingwa (Ottowa), Hoon Choi
(Korean), James Comarell (Greek), Lynn
DePaula (Portuguese), Ketan Dholakia
(Gujarati), Richard O. Effiong (Nigerian),
Nayereh Fallahi (Persian), Angela Fields
(Hopi, Chemehuevi), Gary Fields (Lakota,
Cree), Siri Veslemoy Fluge (Norwegian),
Katalin Forrai (Hungarian), Renee Galagos
(Swedish), Linda Goodman, Judith A. Gray,
Savyasachi Gupta (Marati), Elizabeth Haile
(Shinnecock), Mary Harouny (Persian),
Charlotte Heth (Cherokee), Tim Hunt
(Vietnamese), Marcela Janko (Czech), Raili
Jeffrey (Finnish), Rita Jensen (Danish), Teddy
Kaiahura (Swahili), Gueen Kalaw (Tagalog),
Merehau Kamai (Tahitian), Richard Keeling,
Masanori Kimura (Japanese), Chikahide
Komura (Japanese), Saul Korewa (Hebrew),
Jagadishwar Kota (Tamil), Sokun Koy
(Cambodian), Craig Kurumada (Balkan),
Cindy Trong Le (Vietnamese), Dongchoon Lee
(Korean), Young-Jing Lee (Korean), Nomi Lob
(Hebrew), Sam Loeng (Mandarin, Malay),
Georgia Magpie (Comanche), Mladen Marič
(Croatian), Kuinise Matagi (Samoan), Hiromi
Matsushita (Japanese), Jackie Maynard
(Hawaiian), David McAllester, Mike
Kanathohare McDonald (Mohawk),
Khumbulani Mdlefshe (Zulu), Martin Mkize
(Xhosa), David Montgomery (Turkish), Kazadi
Big Musungayi (Swahili), Professor Akiya
Nakamara (Japanese), Edwin Napia (Maori),
Hang Nguyen (Vietnamese), Richard Nielsen
(Danish), Wil Numkena (Hopi), Eva Ochoa
(Spanish), Drora Oren (Hebrew), Jackie
Osherow (Yiddish), Mavis Oswald (Russian),
Dr. Dil Parkinson (Arabic), Kenny Tahawisoren
Perkins (Mohawk), Alvin Petersen (Sotho),
Phay Phan (Cambodian), Charlie Phim
(Cambodian), Aroha Price (Maori), Marg Puiri
(Samoan), John Rainer (Taos Pueblo, Creek),
Lillian Rainer (Taos Pueblo, Creek, Apache),
Winton Ria (Maori), Arnold Richardson
(Haliwa-Saponi), Thea Roscher (German),
Dr. Wayne Sabey (Japanese), Regine Saintil
(Bamboula Creole), Luci Scherzer (German),
Ken Sekaquaptewa (Hopi), Samouen Seng
(Cambodian), Pei Shin (Mandarin), Dr. Larry
Shumway (Japanese), Gwen Shunatona
(Pawnee, Otoe, Potawatomi), Ernest Siva
(Cahuilla, Serrano [Maringa']), Ben Snowball
(Inuit), Dr. Michelle Stott (German), Keiko
Tanefuji (Japanese), James Taylor
(Portuguese), Shiu-wai Tong (Mandarin),
Tom Toronto (Lao, Thai), Lynn Tran
(Vietnamese), Gulavadee Vaz (Thai), Chen
Ying Wang (Taiwanese), Masakazu Watabe
(Japanese), Freddy Wheeler (Navajo), Keith
Yackeyonny (Comanche), Liming Yang
(Mandarin), Edgar Zurita (Andean)

CONTENTS

284 Celebrations

340 Music Library

UNIT 1

united

CHORUS OF THE WORLD

If you look around
You can hear a sound
Of a great big chorus's song.
It is not of sadness,
It is not of badness,
It's of love, and it's never wrong.

Every mouth sings it loud,
Everyone is very proud.
We are singing
    in the chorus of the world.
All the nations sing together,
All the people now are gathered
To sing the song
    about a nation of the world.

—*Anat Blum, Israeli Student*

by music

Moving Together

Have you ever been at a musical or sports event where the crowd started clapping the beat together? Did you join in? Showing the beat together is a way people can be united by music.

EXPLORE ways to show the beat with "Get Up!"

GET UP!

Words and Music by Teresa Jennings

Get up! Get on your feet! Ev'-ry-bod-y up! Gon-na

move to the beat! Get up! Get on your feet! Ev'-ry-bod-y up! Gon-na

Second time to Coda

move to the beat! Here it is! Do you

feel it? O, yeah! Stomp your feet! Clap your hands!

Raise up your knees like a march-ing band! Lean to the left,

In "Get Up!" there are two beats in each measure. This is shown by the $\frac{2}{4}$ meter signature.

PAT-CLAP with the beat as you listen again. Each pat will be on a strong, stressed beat, and each clap will be on a weak, unstressed beat. This will show the meter.

PROCESSIONALS FROM AROUND THE WORLD

All over the world, people have processions and parades for special occasions. Music for one of these occasions is called a **processional.** What processions can you name?

Music for processions and parades usually has a steady **beat** that helps people to march or walk together. Although a musical beat is steady, like a heartbeat, the speed of the beat can change. The speed of the beat, or **tempo,** can become faster or slower. *Tempo* is an Italian word meaning "time."

LISTENING

Montage of Processionals

LISTENING MAP *Follow the map as you hear processionals from around the world. Listen to the rhythms, feel the beat, and notice the changes in tempo. Also listen to the different* **rhythms,** *or combinations of longer and shorter sounds and silences.*

5 Northern Plains, U.S.A.

8 England

1 United States 2 Italy 3 Bolivia 4 New Orleans, U.S.A. 5 Northern Plains, U.S.A. 6 Philippines 7 Western Africa 8 England

N
W   E
S

7 Western Africa

3 Bolivia

1 United States

4 New Orleans, U.S.A.

6 Philippines

2 Italy

THINK IT THROUGH

What effect does music have on the way people move in a group? How is this different from moving in a group without music?

Here's a song about how people can be united by music.

FEEL the beat as you listen to the song.

DECIDE whether the tempo is slow, medium, or fast.

Words and Music by Garry Smith

Chil - dren, sing all o - ver the place.

Mu - sic brings us to - geth - er!

A hap - py song brings a smile to your face.

Mu - sic brings us to - geth - er! Sing a song loud and clear, for ev' - ry - one to

Woody Guthrie

Some songs seem to draw people together. "This Land Is Your Land" is one of them. It was written by Woody Guthrie, a folk singer and composer. Guthrie traveled all over the United States and wrote more than a thousand songs about the land and its people. Some of his songs helped people lift their spirits during times of hardship.

LISTEN and watch for upward and downward movement in this famous song.

This Land Is Your Land

Words and Music
by Woody Guthrie

This land is your land,___ this land is my land,___

From Cal - i - for - nia___ to the New York is - land,___

From the red-wood for - est___ to the Gulf Stream wa - ters;___

This land was made for you and me.

Verse

1. As I was walk-ing___ that rib-bon of high-way,___
2. I've roamed and ram-bled___ and I fol-lowed my foot-steps___
3. When the sun comes shin-ing___ and I___ was stroll-ing,___

I saw a-bove me___ that end-less sky-way.___
To the spar-kling sands of___ her dia-mond des-erts,___
And the wheat fields wav-ing___ and the dust clouds roll-ing,___

I saw be-low me___ that gold-en val-ley,___
And all a-round me___ a voice was sound-ing,___
As the fog was lift-ing___ a voice was chant-ing,___

D.C. (Last time al Fine)

This land was made for you and me.
"This land was made for you and me."
"This land was made for you and me."

The highness or lowness of a sound is its **pitch**. When you sing a **melody**, you are singing a pattern of pitches that move upward or downward, or stay the same.

You can help yourself learn to read music by noticing **melodic direction**, the way that a melody moves.

9

In the early days of our country, life was hard for many people. Still, they made time for singing and dancing. Making music together was an important part of many gatherings. Before the days of compact discs and television, a song like "We Will Raise a Ruckus Tonight" was passed along from person to person by singing.

TRACE the melodic direction of this African American jubilee as you listen to the song.

We Will Raise a Ruckus Tonight

African American Jubilee
Adapted By René Boyer-White

With Jubilation

G — C — G

Come a - long, you chil - dren, come a - long

G — C — D7

While the moon is shin - ing bright to - night.

G — C — G

Come a - long, you chil - dren, come a - long.

G — D7 — G

We will raise a ruck - us to - night.

In the **score**, or written music, for "We Will Raise a Ruckus Tonight," the direction of the melody is tinted. To read the specific pitches, however, you must know the letter names on the five-line **staff**.

The **G clef**, or **treble clef**, shows that a note placed on the second line of the staff is G. Other lines and spaces follow the musical alphabet: A B C D E F G.

FIND G A B on the staff below.

By remembering the position of these three notes, you will be able to figure out the other lines and spaces.

SING "We Will Raise a Ruckus Tonight" with letter names. It should be easy!

Another way to read music is with pitch syllables. "We Will Raise a Ruckus Tonight" uses only the first three steps of the scale: *do re* and *mi*.

do   re   mi

SING "We Will Raise a Ruckus Tonight" with pitch syllables.

Your Voice

A Personal Musical Instrument

When you hear a new recording by your favorite singer, why can you recognize his or her voice immediately? It's because that singer's voice is a unique musical instrument. Like all instruments, it has its own special sound, called **tone color**. Can your family and friends recognize the tone color of your voice?

LISTENING

Don't Worry, Be Happy (excerpt)
by Bobby McFerrin

Bobby McFerrin surprises audiences with the variety of vocal sounds in his performances. His style is unique and shows how a great imagination can expand our ideas about how the voice can be used.

LISTEN to the different vocal sounds in this recording by Bobby McFerrin. How do you think these sounds were created?

The distance from the highest to the lowest pitch you can sing is your vocal **range**. Your voice also has qualities that result from the way you produce the sound. The terms **heavier register** and **lighter register** describe these qualities. Singers usually find it more comfortable to sing the lowest pitches in the heavier register and the highest pitches in the lighter register. By understanding your voice, you will learn how to sing easily over your full range.

Everyone shared music in Bobby McFerrin's family. Both his parents were professional classical singers. Music surrounded Bobby and his sister from the time they were born. It's not surprising that they both became musicians. After studying music in college, Bobby worked as a keyboard player. He has become a popular concert vocalist, and his recordings are big hits all over the world.

LISTEN as Bobby McFerrin tells you about his unique vocal performance style.

Meet
Bobby McFerrin

EXPLORING VOCAL REGISTERS

Any time you speak, shout, or sing, you use your heavier or lighter vocal register or a combination of the two.

SPEAK "Over My Head" in your lower, heavier register, then in your higher, lighter register.

SING "Over My Head" in these registers.

OVER · MY · HEAD

African American Spiritual

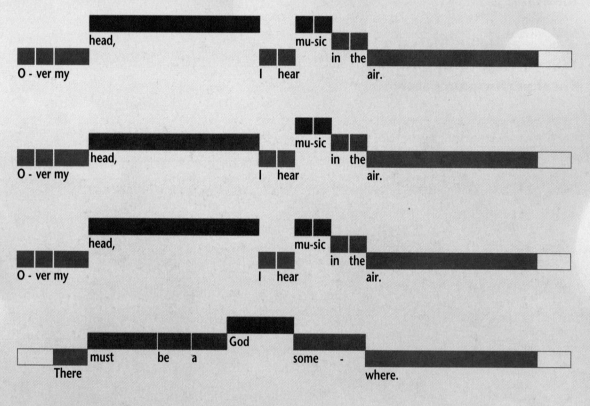

"Over My Head" is an African American spiritual. This melody is
full of expression even though it uses only three pitches.

NAME the pitches at the end of
each phrase.

SING "Over My Head" in your
lighter register.

African American Spiritual

THINK IT THROUGH

How can you show expression as you sing
"Over My Head"?

Peace for all people. . . . Is this one of your hopes for the world? People from many times and places have shared this hope. Folk singer Jean Ritchie has combined an ancient saying with an old melody to create a new song about peace.

Old English Canon
Words by Jean Ritchie
Adapted from Psalm 133:1

What a good-ly thing if the chil-dren of the world could dwell to-geth-er in_____ peace.

COMPARE the range of "Peace Round" to the pitches below. Which part of the song would be easier to sing in the lighter register?

NAME the pitches that are included in both registers.

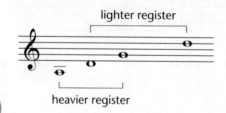

lighter register

heavier register

THINK IT THROUGH
When you sing, what differences do you hear between your lighter and heavier registers?

Hirshhorn Museum and Sculpture Garden, Smithsonian Institution, Gift of Joseph H. Hirshhorn, 1966

HOLY MOUNTAIN III

American artist Horace Pippin created this painting in 1945. Pippin began to paint after he was injured in World War I. At first, he painted war scenes, but later he used subjects from the Bible and scenes of African American family life. In this painting, the artist shows his idea of a perfect world in which people and both wild and tame animals live together in peace.

EVERYBODY LOVES A MELODY

"Ev'rybody Loves Saturday Night" was created at a time when many western African countries were under European rule. During that period, African people in some areas were forbidden to gather at night, except on Saturdays.

This song became popular with musical groups called "highlife bands" in cities throughout western Africa. Later, it became known in other parts of the world. People translated the words of the song into many different languages. Can you add a verse in another language?

Top to bottom:
Ladjii Camara and band, Senegal
O. J. Ekemode and the Nigerian
   Allstars, Nigeria
Les Amazones du Guinea, Guinea

18

EV'RYBODY LOVES SATURDAY NIGHT

Western African Song

Ga: Mɔ - fia mo - ni s'mɔ hɔ gbɛ - kɛ.
Pronunciation: mɔ fia mo ni smɔ hɔ bɛ kɛ
English: Ev' - ry - bod - y loves Sat - ur - day night.

Mɔ - fia mo - ni s'mɔ hɔ gbɛ - kɛ.
mɔ fia mo ni smɔ hɔ bɛ kɛ
Ev' - ry - bod - y loves Sat - ur - day night.

Mɔ- fia mo - ni, mɔ- fia mo- ni, mɔ- fia mo- ni, mɔ- fia mo - ni,
mɔ fia mo ni mɔ fia mo ni mɔ fia mo ni mɔ fia mo ni
Ev'- ry- bod - y, ev'- ry- bod- y, ev'- ry- bod - y, ev'- ry- bod - y,

Mɔ - fia mo - ni s'mɔ hɔ gbɛ - kɛ.
mɔ fia mo ni smɔ hɔ bɛ kɛ
Ev' - ry - bod - y loves Sat - ur - day night.

Highlife bands play western instruments such as drum sets, electric guitars, and Latin percussion, as well as African drums, rattles, and bells. Highlife started in Ghana and Sierra Leone. From there it spread to other African countries and to other parts of the world. The enjoyment of this music unites people from many cultures.

NEW CHALLENGES

STEP-TOUCH to the beat as you sing "Ev'rybody Loves Saturday Night." When you get to the third line, stand and face your partner. Clap on each rest, and give your partner a "high five" on the third syllable of each *ev'rybody*. On the fourth line, move to a new partner with two side-close steps.

1

To do a step-touch, take a step with one foot. Then lightly touch the floor next to it with the other foot, without putting weight on it.

2

Face your partner and clap.

4 To do a side-close, take a step sideways and move the other foot next to it.

3 Give your partner a "high five."

ADD A NEW PART

When you learned "Ev'rybody Loves Saturday Night," everyone sang the melody. This is called singing in **unison.**

Two or more pitches sounding at the same time create **harmony.** At the bottom of the page is a harmony part to sing with the melody of "Ev'rybody Loves Saturday Night." This part includes the pitch F, written in the first space.

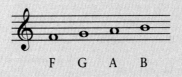

F   G   A   B

TRACE the melodic direction of the harmony part as you listen to it.

IDENTIFY the pitch letter names.

SING the harmony part with pitch syllables. F is *do*.

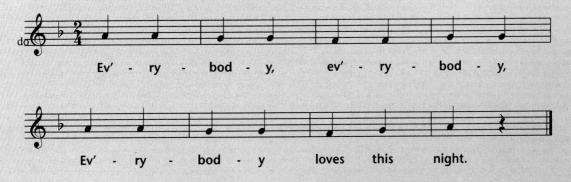

do

Ev' - ry - bod - y,   ev' - ry - bod - y,

Ev' - ry - bod - y   loves   this   night.

Top design based on raffia mat pattern from Zaire. Bottom design based on a mud relief on wall of Nigerian house.

A line near the treble clef connects parts that are sung at the same time. These connected parts form a **system.**

SING this song from a two-part system.

EV'RYBODY LOVES SATURDAY NIGHT

Western African Song

Unison

F   C7   F

Ga: Mɔ - fia mo - ni s'mɔ hɔ gbɛ kɛ.
Pronunciation: mɔ fia mo ni smɔ hɔ bɛ kɛ
English: Ev' - ry - bod - y loves Sat - ur - day night.

F   C7   F

Mɔ - fia mo - ni s'mɔ hɔ gbɛ kɛ.
mɔ fia mo ni smɔ hɔ bɛ kɛ
Ev' - ry - bod - y loves Sat - ur - day night.

Melody F   C7   F   C7

Mɔ - fia mo - ni, mɔ - fia mo - ni, mɔ - fia mo - ni, mɔ - fia mo - ni,
mɔ fia mo ni mɔ fia mo ni mɔ fia mo ni mɔ fia mo ni
Ev' - ry - bod - y, ev' - ry - bod - y, ev' - ry - bod - y, ev' - ry - bod - y,

Harmony

Mɔ - fia mo - ni, mɔ - fia mo - ni,
mɔ fia mo ni mɔ fia mo ni
Ev' - ry - bod - y, ev' - ry - bod - y,

F   C7   F

Mɔ - fia mo - ni s'mɔ hɔ gbɛ - kɛ.
mɔ fia mo ni smɔ hɔ bɛ kɛ
Ev' - ry - bod - y loves Sat - ur - day night.____

Mɔ - fia mo - ni s'mɔ hɔ gbɛ - kɛ.
mɔ fia mo ni smɔ hɔ bɛ kɛ
Ev' - ry - bod - y loves____ this night.

IT'S A MYSTERY TO ME!

The harmony part of "Ev'rybody Loves Saturday Night" uses the pitches F, G, and A. Here is another melody written with only those three pitches. It is a song you have already sung.

PLAY the "Mystery Tune" below. Do you recognize the song?

MYSTERY TUNE

SING the melody with letter names and name the mystery tune.

Remember the clue that helped you solve this mystery: reading the notes!

The border designs are from a Benin bronze sculpture from Nigeria. The three wooden masks are from Nigeria (top left), the Congo (top right), and the Ivory Coast (bottom).

TIME for RHYTHM

Reading pitches helps you to sing a melody you have never heard before. However, to sing or play a melody correctly, you must also be able to read rhythmic notation. Rhythmic **notation** shows you how to perform the long and short sounds and silences that make up a piece of music.

ECHO rhythm patterns you hear as some of your classmates pat to the beat.

LISTEN and decide whether each beat contains one sound, two sounds, or no sound.

Here is rhythm notation for one sound, two sounds, and no sound in a beat.

quarter note	eighth notes	quarter rest
(one sound)	(two sounds)	(no sound)

In music that you play and sing, the **meter,** which is a set of beats, organizes the rhythms. **Bar lines** separate the sets of beats into **measures.** The first beat of each measure is usually stressed more than the other beats.

number of beats in measure

measure

meter signature

quarter gets the beat   measure line   double bar

The **meter signature** tells you the number of beats in a measure and what rhythm value gets the beat. A **double bar** shows the end of the piece.

CLAP the patterns below, reading from notation.

Four times

Four times

A RHYTHM "GET-TOGETHER" IN THE PHILIPPINE ISLANDS

Percussion players all over the world enjoy combining instrumental sounds for exciting rhythmic effects. In the Mindanao Islands of the Philippines, there are musical groups called **kulintang**. The kulintang contains only **percussion** instruments, those played by striking or shaking. The kulintang is made up of gongs and drums. Pictures below and on the next page show the instruments in the kulintang.

The kulintang is the main instrument of the ensemble. It is an 8- to 10-foot row of bronze gongs on which the melody is played. The gongs are of various sizes and produce different pitches.

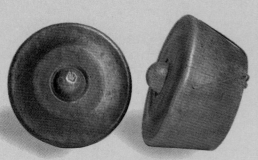

Other large gongs, called agungs, provide the bass part. They are often played by two people. One person plays a pattern. The other person **improvises**, or makes up on the spot, another pattern to play. The improvised pattern is played during the rests of the first person's pattern.

The dabakan, a drum, is struck with two pieces of split bamboo. The dabakan plays a rhythmic accompaniment of faster notes.

The babandir, a small, hand-held gong, often plays a short, repeated pattern, or **ostinato.** Its sharp tone color adds rhythmic "spice" to the ensemble.

Some groups use hanging gongs called gandingan. These gongs play a melodic ostinato that supports the main melody. The frame stands about five feet high.

LISTENING

Adongko Dongko a Gakit

Philippine Kulintang
Wedding Processional

*Like the instruments in a rock band or orchestra, each set of instruments in the kulintang plays a special role in creating the **ensemble**, or group, sound.*

LISTEN for the following patterns, played by an agung, as you listen to the kulintang ensemble. Where have you heard these patterns before?

Four times

Four times

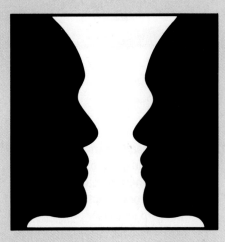

CAN YOU BELIEVE YOUR EYES?

What do you see in the drawing? Close your eyes and look again. Did you see the same thing? This drawing is an optical illusion. You might see it as a vase one time you look, and as two faces when you look again. Can you see both at the same time?

SKY AND WATER I, JUNE 1938

The woodcut *Sky and Water I, June 1938* by M.C. Escher uses positive and negative shapes. The first shape that you see is called a figure, or *positive*, shape. The surrounding area is called the ground, or *negative*, shape. You can shift your eyes between the positive and negative shapes. What do you see?

© 1938 M.C. Escher Cordon Art-Baarn-Holland Collection
Haags Gemeentemuseum, The Hague

CAN YOU BELIEVE YOUR EARS?

When you listened to the kulintang music, you may have noticed a second rhythm blending in with the pattern you were clapping. The second agung, which has a slightly higher sound than the first one, played this rhythm. The second instrument fills in all the rests in the first instrument's pattern.

THINK IT THROUGH

How are the agung parts of the kulintang music like the art above?

THE POSITIVE-NEGATIVE GAME

Here is a rhythm echo game to help you learn to play music in the style of the Philippine kulintang ensemble.

READ the first line below. Say *gong* for each note in the first line. This line is the same as the rhythm patterns you have been practicing.

PRACTICE clapping each note in the second line. Form two groups. Have each group do one of the lines.

READ both lines yourself. Be your own echo! This time, you will speak the first line and clap the second line. This is the first half of the song.

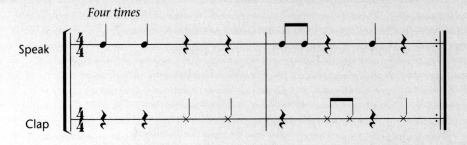

PLAY the other pattern you have practiced. Use the same echo style. This is the second half of the song.

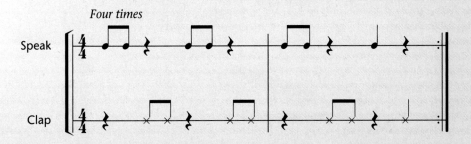

PERFORM the patterns with "Adongko Dongko a Gakit."

PERCUSSION

The instruments that you heard in the Philippine kulintang ensemble are all part of the percussion family. The sound of percussion instruments is made by two objects striking one another. The objects may be struck directly together, or one object may be scraped, shaken, rubbed, plucked, or struck with the hand or a mallet.

Here are some percussion instruments you may have seen, heard, or played. How is sound produced with each of them?

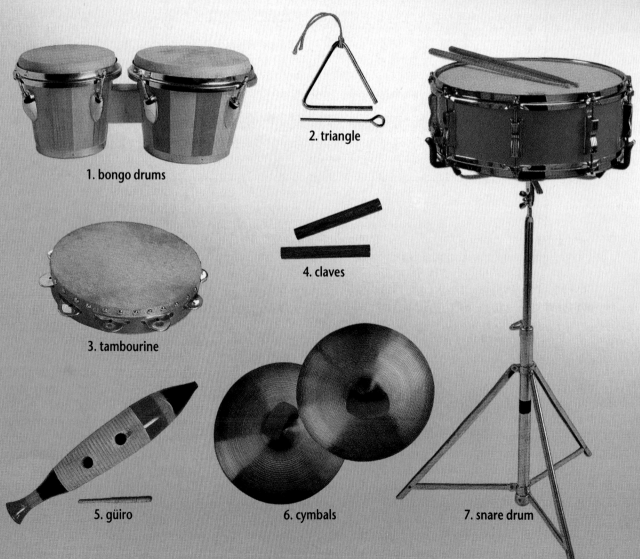

1. bongo drums

2. triangle

3. tambourine

4. claves

5. güiro

6. cymbals

7. snare drum

INSTRUMENTS

SOURCES FOR MUSICAL SOUNDS

Most percussion instruments began from simple sound sources. At first, people used natural materials and objects that they found around them. The first maracas were made from dried gourds filled with seeds or other small objects that rattle.

maracas

It's easy to see where the log drum came from!

log drum

Percussion instruments can be created from many everyday objects. Where might instruments such as the cowbell, the claves, and the güiro have come from?

LOOK for objects in your classroom that might be used as percussion instruments.

THINK IT THROUGH

When are sounds musical and when are they noise? Think of a noise. How can you change it to make it more musical?

MAKING PERCUSSION MUSIC TOGETHER

You have already practiced the rhythms you need to play along with the kulintang ensemble.

PLAY the drum and cowbell with "Adongko Dongko a Gakit" using the patterns below.

kulintang ensemble

IT'S MORE THAN RHYTHM

The kulintang ensemble plays more than rhythm. The gongs play melodies as well. You can play the melody of "Adongko Dongko a Gakit." Some of the sounds in the melody are two beats long. In $\frac{4}{4}$ meter, a sound that lasts for two beats is shown with a **half note** ($\,\flat$). A **half rest** ($-$) shows a silence for the same length as a half note.

FIND the half notes and half rests in the score below.

PRACTICE clapping the rhythm of the melody. Use a clap-slide for the half notes.

ADONGKO DONGKO A GAKIT

Philippine Kulintang
Wedding Processional

TAIWAN

PHILIPPINES

• Mindanao

Resonator bells

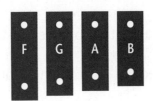

PRACTICE singing this melody with letter names, and then practice playing the melody.

COMBINE the drum, cowbell, and resonator-bell parts to form a *percussion ensemble.*

Find That Phrase

A piece of music is a bit like a story or a mosaic. All are made up of small ideas that combine to make larger ones. In a story, the small idea is the sentence. In music, a complete thought or idea is called a **phrase.** Phrases are combined to form a longer piece of music. In "Over My Head," the first phrase is this:

O - ver my head,_____ I hear mu- sic in the air._____

SING the entire song. How many phrases do you hear?

You can figure out how a piece of music is put together by noticing if the phrases are the same, almost the same, or different. Small letters can be used to label phrases.

The first phrase is called a . If any other phrase is exactly

the same as the first, it is also called a . If the next phrase is

almost the same, it is called a' (*a* prime). If the next phrase is

really different, it is called .

34

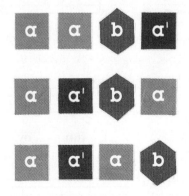

FIND THAT FORM

The sentences in a story must be put together in an orderly form for the story to make sense. This is also true of music—phrases must be put together in an orderly way. Here are some ways phrases can be put together to make a musical form.

a a b a'

a a' b a

a a' a b

Do these forms match any songs you know?
Which one matches the form of "Over My Head"?

FIND THAT SECTION

Musical phrases can be combined into larger **sections** that have more than one musical idea. Each section is identified by a capital letter. "Side by Side" has four sections. Its form is A A B A. Many other popular songs have this form.

THINK about how the B section is different from the A sections as you learn "Side by Side."

Words and Music by Harry Woods

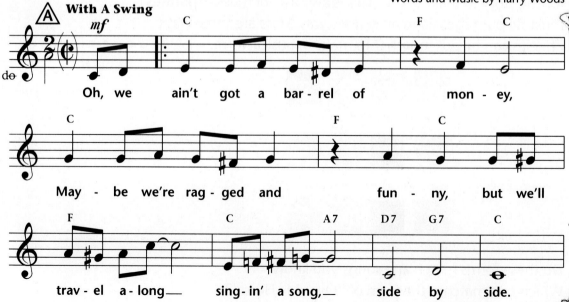

With A Swing

Oh, we ain't got a bar-rel of mon-ey,

May-be we're rag-ged and fun-ny, but we'll

trav-el a-long sing-in' a song, side by side.

TEXTURE IN MUSIC

If you could touch these pieces of cloth, you might say that the example on the bottom felt rough or thick, while the example on the top felt smooth or thin. These words describe the texture of the fabric.

Art also has texture. Notice the textures of the two oil paintings, *Abstract No. 2* by Lee Krasner and *Winter Road I* by Georgia O'Keeffe. Which has a thin texture? Which has a thick texture?

DESCRIBE other art you have seen with a thick or a thin texture.

The words *thick* and *thin* can also be used to describe texture in music. Musical **texture** is the sound created by different pitches, rhythms, and tone colors played or sung together. Just as there are many kinds of form in music, there are many kinds of texture.

Lee Krasner, ABSTRACT NO. 2 1946–1948
Robert Miller Gallery, NY

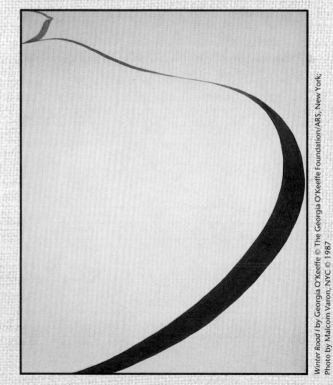

Winter Road I by Georgia O'Keeffe © The Georgia O'Keeffe Foundation/ARS, New York;
Photo by Malcom Varon, NYC © 1987

When a single melody is played or sung, the texture is thin.

When many parts are heard at the same time, the texture is thicker. Adding a musical background, or **accompaniment**, to a melody makes the texture thicker.

Listening to the Nightingale

Listening to the nightingale singing
among the flowers
or to the cry of the frog which dwells
in the water,
we recognize the truth
that of all living things
there is not one
which does not utter song.

—Ki Tsurayuki

Accompaniments can be created from both instrumental and vocal sounds.

SELECT percussion sounds to play as an accompaniment. Play the percussion sounds while a classmate speaks.

CREATE a background of vocal sounds. Include the sounds of birds and animals mentioned in the poem.

THINK IT THROUGH
How did each accompaniment add to the meaning of the poem? How would the texture change if both accompaniments were heard at the same time?

Change the musical texture to enrich
a song you already know. How does
the texture change in the refrain?

Words and Music by Garry Smith

1. Chil - dren, sing   all   o - ver   the   place.___
2. Sing   a   song   to   bright - en your day.___

Mu - sic brings us   to - geth   -   er!
Mu - sic brings us   to - geth   -   er!

A   hap - py   song brings a   smile to your face.___
Sing it   at   work   or___   sing   it   at   play.___

A **canon,** or round, has a melody that is imitated in one or more parts. Each time a new part is added, the texture becomes thicker.

Peace Round

Old English Canon
Words by Jean Ritchie
Adapted from Psalm 133:1

MUSIC THAT UNITES

When friends get together, there's often music in the air. Sing "Get Up!" and think about the title of this unit, "United by Music." What kept you together when you all were singing and moving? It was the music—most noticeably, the beat and the rhythm of the music.

The ideas expressed in the words of a song can also unite people. The message of "This Land Is Your Land" has united people all over the country since it was first sung by Woody Guthrie. As you sing this song, notice the upward movement of the melody at the beginning of most phrases.

Singing with a group, whether it is in unison or in harmony, unites people through a shared experience. Sing "We Will Raise a Ruckus Tonight" in unison or "Ev'rybody Loves Saturday Night" in unison or with the harmony part.

Watching television or a movie, attending a baseball game or a party, listening to the radio, participating in religious services—think about all of the things you do, and then think about them without music. It's almost impossible to imagine. Music is with us everywhere. Sing "Music Brings Us Together!"

CHECK IT OUT

1. Which rhythm do you hear?

   a.

   b.

   c.

   d.

2. Choose the melodic direction that you hear.

   a. ↗   b. ↘   c. ↘ ↗   d. →

3. Choose the melodic direction that you hear.

   a. ↗   b. ↘   c. ↘ ↗   d. →

4. Choose the melodic direction that you hear.

   a. ↗   b. ↘   c. ↘ ↗   d. →

5. Which example shows the pitches you hear?

   a.   c.

   b.   d.

6. Which example shows the pitches you hear?

   a.   c.

   b.   d.

CREATE

Make a Melody

Choose ♩, ♫, and 𝄽 to fill four measures in ⁴⁄₄ meter. The last beat should be a quarter rest.

Play the first two measures on a percussion instrument or found sound, and the last two measures on a contrasting percussion instrument or found sound. For example, you could use a hand drum and woodblocks or a desk and radiator.

CREATE a melody by choosing pitches for your rhythms. Use the pitches F G A or G A B. If you use F G A, end on F. If you use G A B, end on G.

PLAY your melody on resonator bells or other pitched instruments.

Write

In your family or community, when is music performed? Write a brief description of an event you have attended that included music or an experience you had performing music. In what way did the music help to bring people together?

OUR HANDS, OUR HEARTS

A traditional Native American worldview is that the earth is like a caring mother. The earth provides everything needed to survive. It provides food, water, medicine, and materials to make beautiful and useful housing, clothing, and tools. The elements and the living things of the earth also teach important lessons about life. Native Americans believe that people should respect and care for the earth because of all that it gives and teaches us. This respect for the earth is shown in many Native American songs and dances.

The photographs of the Zuni family, pueblo, and jar all date from the early 1900s. The pieces of jewelry pictured are modern Zuni designs.

READ "Song of the Skyloom."
How does this poem explain
the relationship between
people and nature?

SONG of the SKYLOOM

Oh our Mother the Earth, oh our Father the Sky,

Your children are we, and with tired backs

We bring you the gifts that you love.

Then weave for us a garment of brightness;

May the weft be the red light of evening,

May the fringes be the falling rain,

May the border be the standing rainbow.

Thus weave for us a garment of brightness

That we may walk fittingly where birds sing,

That we may walk fittingly where grass is green,

Oh our Mother the Earth, oh our Father the Sky!

—from *Songs of the Tewa*

How the Fawn Got its Spots

The following Lakota legend tells how some animals are protected from their natural enemies. As you read the legend, think of instrumental sounds that might represent the animals mentioned.

Long ago, when the world was new, Wakan Tanka, The Great Mystery, was walking around. As he walked, he spoke to himself of the many things he had done to help the four-legged ones and the birds survive.

"It is good," Wakan Tanka said. "I have given Mountain Lion sharp claws and Grizzly Bear great strength. It is much easier now for them to survive. I have given Wolf sharp teeth and I have given his little brother, Coyote, quick wits. It is much easier now for them to survive. I have given Beaver a flat tail and webbed feet to swim beneath the water and teeth which can cut down the trees and I have given slow-moving Porcupine quills to protect itself. Now it is easier for them to survive. I have given the birds their feathers and the ability to fly so that they may escape their enemies. I have given speed to the deer and the rabbit so that it will be hard for their enemies to catch them. Truly it is now much easier for them to survive."

However, as Wakan Tanka spoke, a mother deer came up to him. Behind her was her small fawn, wobbling on weak legs.

"Great One," she said. "It is true that you have given many gifts to the four-leggeds and the winged ones to help them survive. It is true that you gave me great speed and now my enemies find it hard to catch me. My speed is a great protection, indeed. But what of my little one here? She does not yet have speed. It is easy for our enemies, with their sharp teeth and their claws, to catch her. If my children do not survive, how can my people live?"

"Wica yaka pelo!" said Wakan Tanka. "You have spoken truly; you are right. Have your little one come here and I will help."

Then Wakan Tanka made paint from the earth and the plants. He painted spots upon the fawn's body so that, when she lay still, her color blended in with the earth and she could not be seen. Then Wakan Tanka breathed upon her, taking away her scent.

"Now," Wakan Tanka said, "your little ones will always be safe if they only remain still when they are away from your side. None of your enemies will see your little ones or be able to catch their scent."

So it has been from that day on. When a young deer is too small and weak to run swiftly, it is covered with spots that blend in with the earth. It has no scent and it remains very still and close to the earth when its mother is not by its side. And when it has grown enough to have the speed Wakan Tanka gave its people, then it loses those spots it once needed to survive.

LISTENING

Zuni Sunrise Song

"Zuni Sunrise Song" is a morning greeting song. It expresses respect for nature.

This musical greeting occurs several times in the song.

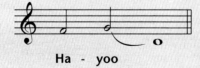

Ha - yoo

The singer also addresses the Zuni people, calling them *Shiwona*.

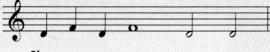

Shee - wa - yoo - wa - o - na

from
African Dance

The low beating of the tom-toms,
The slow beating of the tom-toms,
Low...slow
Slow...low
Stirs your blood.

—*Langston Hughes*

DRUMS!

You've had the experience: someone turns on the radio and you find yourself "drumming" on your chair. It's not anything you learn. You just do it. It's the power of rhythm at work!

LISTENING

Drum Montage

LISTEN to drumming from many parts of the world in "Drum Montage."

MOVE in a different way each time you hear a new drum sound and style begin.

2 Bata drum from Nigeria

◀ **1** Drum set from the United States

4 Tabla from North India ▽

Taiko drums from Japan **3** ▽

5 Conga drum from South America

54

"Funga Alafia" is a greeting song from western Africa. If you were to hear it performed by African musicians, you most certainly would hear drums.

PLAY drums on the beat as you sing this song.

FUNGA ALAFIA

Western African Welcome Dance

Fun-ga a-la-fia. Ah-shay, Ah-shay. Fun-ga a-la-fia. Ah-shay, Ah-shay.

Pronunciation: fʊng a a la fya a she a she   fʊng a a la fya a she a she

B *Spoken freely*
With my thoughts, I welcome you.
With my words, I welcome you.
With my heart, I welcome you.
See? I have nothing up my sleeve.

How many times do you see this rhythm ♪ ♩   ♪ ?

EXPRESS the B section of the song with gestures and speech.

1. With my thoughts,

2. I welcome you.

3. With my words,

4. I welcome you.

5. With my heart,

6. I welcome you.

7. See? I have nothing up my sleeve.

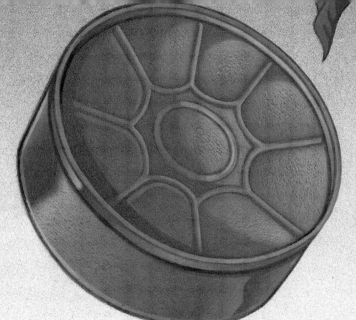

In Jamaica, where this calypso song was created, old oil barrels are made into pitched **steel drums.** They play both rhythm and melody.

Mango Walk

Jamaican Calypso

do

C7   F

My moth-er deed-a tell me that you go man-go walk,

C7   F

you go man-go walk, you go man-go walk.

C7   F

My moth-er deed-a tell me that you go man-go walk

C7   F

and eat all the num-ber 'lev-en.

COMPARE the rhythm of the tinted measures with the rhythm of *ahshay, ahshay* in "Funga Alafia."

DRUMMING RIGHT ALONG

Drums are everywhere. Look around. What drums do you see—floor, desk, radiator, chair, book, your lap? Some famous drummers started out playing on the streets using the bottoms of plastic buckets!

A rhythm pattern consists of long and short sounds and silences, usually with an underlying steady beat. **Syncopation** is a type of rhythm in which some stressed notes come between beats instead of on beats.

PLAY these patterns on a drum and tell which has syncopation. If you don't have an actual drum, use something else.

Go man - go walk

Moth - er deed - a tell me that you

THE POWER of SONG

Imagine being a slave on a cotton plantation in 1850. You are working in the fields when you hear soft voices singing "This train is bound for glory. . . ." You add your voice to the song, and that night, under cover of darkness, you and several others begin your escape to freedom. This song was a code song, one of many that pointed the way to freedom in the North.

This Train

African American Spiritual

1. This train is bound for glo - ry, this train,____
2. This train don't car - ry no gam - blers, this train,____
3. This train is bound for glo - ry, this train,____

This train is bound for glo - ry, this train,____
This train don't car - ry no gam - blers, this train,____
This train is bound for glo - ry, this train,____

This train is bound for glo - ry, If you ride it, you
This train don't car - ry no gam - blers, No hy - po - crites,____ no
This train is bound for glo - ry, Don't car - ry noth - ing but the

must be ho - ly, This train is bound for glo - ry, this train.____
mid - night ram - blers, This train is bound for glo - ry, this train.____
right-teous and the ho - ly, This train is bound for glo - ry, this train.____

PENTATONIC: A FIVE-TONE SCALE

The folk song "This Train" uses the pitches *do re mi so la*. A folk song usually ends on its **tonal center**, or resting place. For "This Train," the tonal center is *do*.

The pitches of "This Train" are based on a **scale**, which is an ordered series of pitches. You can form a scale by placing the pitches from any song in order from lowest to highest or highest to lowest. A common **pentatonic scale** includes the five pitches *do re mi so la*. The pentatonic scale may include higher or lower pitches, and it may start on any pitch, letter name, or syllable.

CHOOSE the example that matches the pitches in "This Train," and you'll see how this works.

PLAY and sing these pentatonic scales.

do re mi   so la
F   G   A   C   D

so₁ la₁   do re mi   so la
D   E   G   A   B   D   E

do re mi   so la   do'
C   D   E   G   A   C

VIEWING MOUNTAINS IN YÜ-HANG (detail)
Landscapes are important subjects in Chinese painting. This landscape was painted by Shih-t'au, who lived from 1642 to 1707.

GAU SHAN CHING
ALI MOUNTAIN

The view is breathtaking: mountain peaks rising from the mist, lush green trees, the rush of a mountain stream, and the scent of jasmine in the air. A swallow swoops above as you watch the changing clouds. Do you have a place like this to visit? In Taiwan, people enjoy the peace of Ali Mountain.

Taiwanese Folk Song
English Words by Marilyn Davidson
and Judy Bond

Mandarin: 高 山 青
Pronunciation: ga u sha n ching
English: A - li moun - tain's so green.

涧 水 藍
jyɛ n shwe lan
Near a stream so blue.

阿 里 山 的 姑 娘 美 如 水
a li shan da gu niang me ru shwe
A - li moun - tain peo - ple, love - ly to see.

阿　里　山　的　少　年　壮　　如　山
a　li　shan　da　shau　niɛn　tjuang　　ru　shan
A - li moun - tain dan - cers, grace - ful and strong.

啊
a
Ah!

啊
a
Ah!

This song includes these pitches. The D and E are used at both high and low pitch levels.

D E G A B D E
so₁ la₁ do re mi so la

COMPARE the notes in "Gau Shan Ching" with these pitches. What pitches are used in each phrase? How are the phrases alike and different?

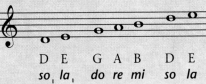

RHYTHM

IT'S CLEARLY POPULAR

Popular music is what you're likely to hear wherever you go. Back in the 1920s and 1930s, some of the most popular songs came from the pens of George Gershwin and his brother, Ira. They wrote many of these songs for musicals.

A **musical** features a story told with singing, drama, and dancing. *Oklahoma, The Wiz, The Sound of Music, West Side Story, Phantom of the Opera,* and *Grease* are all famous musicals that have played on Broadway. Many musicals have been made into movies. The Gershwin brothers wrote "I Got Rhythm" in the 1930s for their musical *Girl Crazy*. Ethel Merman, a famous singer of that time, made the song a hit.

I GOT RHYTHM

Music by George Gershwin
Words by Ira Gershwin

FORM: IT HOLDS THOSE SONGS TOGETHER

Have you ever listened to songs that were popular when your grandparents were your age? Why are some of these songs still appealing? It might be great rhythm or a singable melody, or it might be something else that can make a song easy to learn—an easy-to-follow form.

"I Got Rhythm" and "Side by Side," along with many other songs, have the same form. It's A A B A—the form most often used in American popular music.

Ⓐ The first A section is a melody with one set of words.

Ⓐ The second A section is the same melody with different words.

Ⓑ The B section has a different melody and words.

Ⓐ The last A section is like the first, with different words. The ending is sometimes changed by adding extra measures, called the **tag.** "I Got Rhythm" has this kind of ending.

LISTENING

I Got Rhythm (xylophone version)
by George Gershwin

Jazz is a type of popular music. It began in the United States in the early 1900s and is enjoyed all over the world today. Jazz musicians often improvise around known songs and forms such as "I Got Rhythm" and A A B A form.

LISTEN for the A A B A form in this jazz version of "I Got Rhythm."

PAT to the beat with alternating hands during the A section.

Acrylic and fabric on canvas 90" × 96" Collection: Dr. and Mrs. Acinapura Courtesy Steinbaum Krauss Gallery, NYC

PAS DE DEUX

Pas de Deux means "Step by Two." The painting was created by Miriam Schapiro in 1986. It is made up of both acrylic and fabric. This painting shows energy through the use of color and objects in motion. Where might these dancers be?

"The Rhythm of Life" is a song from *Sweet Charity*, a musical written in 1966. The music has a bold, energetic style.

LISTEN to "The Rhythm of Life." Are there any syncopated patterns in this song?

COMPARE the sections. Is the song in A A B A form?

THE RHYTHM OF LIFE

Music by Cy Coleman
Words by Dorothy Fields (Adapted)

When I start-ed down the street last Sun-day, Feel-in' might-y low and kind-a mean, Sud-den-ly a voice said, "Go forth, neigh-bor! Spread the pic-ture on a wid-er screen!" And the voice said, "Neigh-bor, there's a mil-lion rea-sons Why you should be glad in all four sea-sons! Hit the road, neigh-bor, leave your wor-ries and strife! Spread the re-li-gion of the rhy-thm of life." For the

get the beat

In many parts of the world, if there's music, there's movement. In this scene of Jamaican musicians, the steel drummer feels the rhythm throughout her body. The listeners are just as involved. They're dancing, caught up in the power of rhythm.

in your feet!

MOVE to "Mango Walk," a Jamaican folk song, using the steps listed. After some practice, you'll probably be able to move as you sing the song. Even though many of the song rhythms are syncopated, you will be stepping on the steady beat.

DANCE STEPS

1. four steps forward
2. side-close-side, touch (moving to one side)
3. side-close-side, touch (moving to the other side)
4. three steps circling in place, touch
5. four steps backward
6. side-close-side, touch
7. side-close-side, touch
8. stamp, three claps

START

touch

left   right

MOVE facing a partner to really get into the calypso spirit. Move in the same or opposite directions.

TIE IT ALL TOGETHER

A sound that lasts for one beat can be written in two ways: ♩ or ♫

A **tie** (‿) is a musical sign that joins two notes of the same pitch. The tie combines the two notes into a single sound equal to their total **duration** (length).

LISTEN and echo-clap or play the patterns below.

How do the ties make the patterns sound syncopated?

hand drum

The syncopated pattern ♪♩♪ (tied) can also be written as ♪♩♪

LISTEN for the sound of ♪♩♪ as you clap or play these patterns.

COMPARE them to the tied patterns on page 70.

CREATE your own composition with syncopation. Make up new patterns or choose two or three of the patterns above. Then decide how to combine them.

PLAY your rhythms on a drum while a classmate plays on the beat with another percussion instrument. Trade parts.

claves

"Sweet Potatoes" and "Mango Walk" have the same form and meter, but their rhythm patterns are completely different.

LISTEN for ♩. ♫ ♩ | ♩ in "Sweet Potatoes."

Sweet Potatoes

Louisiana Creole Folk Song

do

1. Soon as we all cook sweet po - ta - toes,
2. Soon as sup - per's gone, Mam - ma calls us,
3. Soon's we touch our heads to the pil - low,
4. Soon's the roost - er crow in the morn - ing,

sweet po - ta - toes, sweet po - ta - toes.
Mam - ma calls us, Mam - ma calls us.
to the pil - low, to the pil - low.
in the morn - ing, in the morn - ing.

Soon as we all cook sweet po - ta - toes,
Soon as sup - per's gone, Mam - ma calls us,
Soon's we touch our heads to the pil - low,
Soon's the roost - er crow in the morn - ing,

Eat 'em while they're hot.
Get a - long to bed.
Go to sleep right smart!
Got - ta wash our face.

A **dotted quarter note** (𝅘𝅥𝅭) is equal in length to one quarter note plus one eighth note.

PRACTICE clapping these patterns.

SING "Sweet Potatoes" and "Mango Walk" at the same time. Notice how the two tunes and their different rhythms fit together.

Folk songs such as "Mango Walk" and "Sweet Potatoes" are often accompanied with percussion instruments. Many of these instruments can be made from everyday objects such as gourds or discarded oil drums.

SAY the words as you practice the rhythms below.

PLAY the patterns on percussion instruments.

ACCOMPANY "Mango Walk" with instruments.

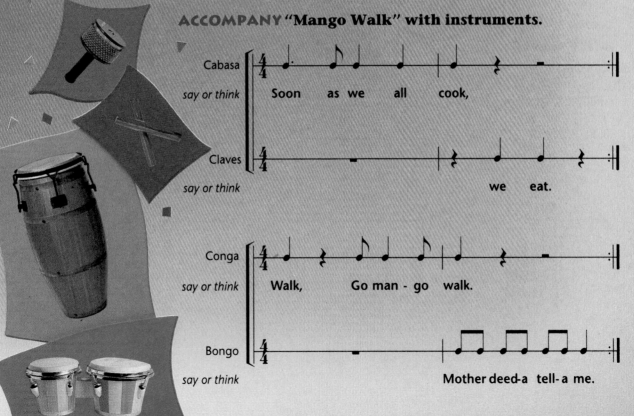

Cabasa

say or think Soon as we all cook,

Claves

say or think we eat.

Conga

say or think Walk, Go man - go walk.

Bongo

say or think Mother deed-a tell-a me.

PARTNERS

"Sweet Potatoes" and "Mango Walk" can be sung as **partner songs**. They are separate songs, but they sound good when sung at the same time. "Sweet Potatoes" also has a **countermelody**, a contrasting melody written to go with a song.

CLAP the rhythm pattern in the countermelody that is also found in "Sweet Potatoes."

The first pitch in the countermelody is C. The first pitch in the melody is high C (C'). What are the pitch letter names of the notes in both of these melodies? Are there notes in one song that are not sung in the other?

SING the countermelody together with "Sweet Potatoes," reading the notation below.

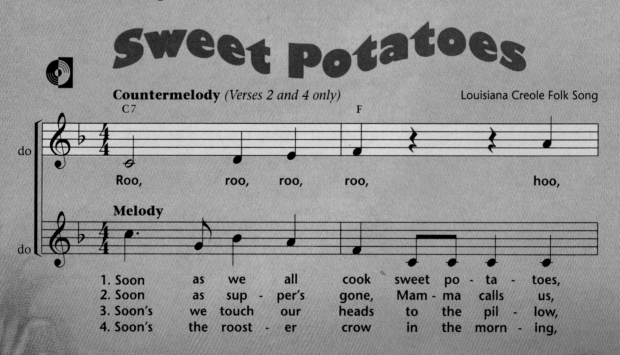

Sweet Potatoes

Countermelody (Verses 2 and 4 only)

Louisiana Creole Folk Song

Roo,   roo, roo, roo,   hoo,

Melody

1. Soon as we all cook sweet po - ta - toes,
2. Soon as sup - per's gone, Mam - ma calls us,
3. Soon's we touch our heads to the pil - low,
4. Soon's the roost - er crow in the morn - ing,

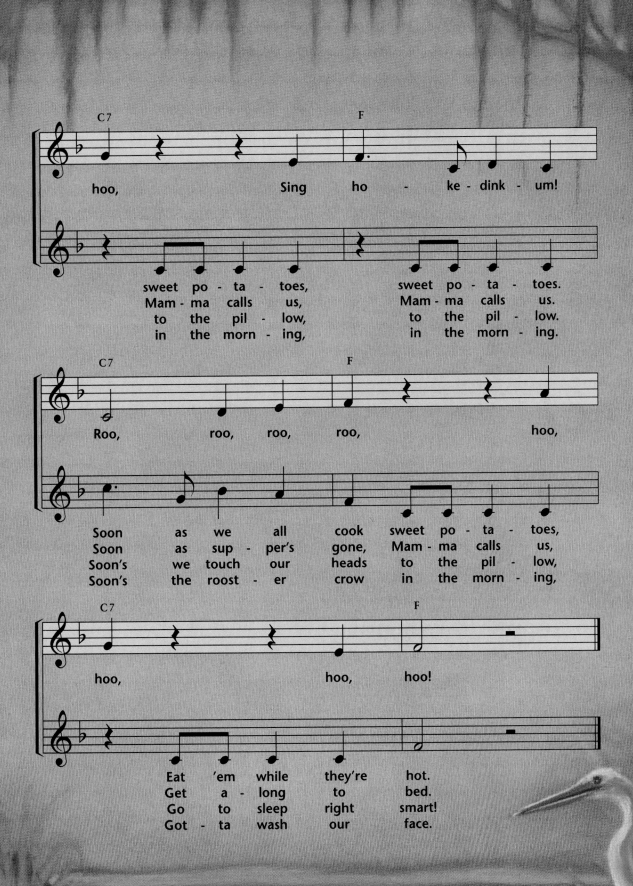

SING all three melodies together.

Louisiana Creole Folk Song
and Jamaican Calypso

Sweet Potatoes

Soon as we all cook sweet po-ta-toes, sweet po-ta-toes, sweet po-ta-toes.

Countermelody

Roo, roo, roo, roo, hoo, hoo,

Mango Walk

My moth-er deed-a tell me that you go man-go walk, you go man-go walk, you go man-go walk. My

Sing ho-ke-dink-um!

Soon as we all cook sweet po-ta-toes,

Roo, roo, roo, roo, hoo,

moth-er deed-a tell me that you go man-go walk and

Eat 'em while they're hot.

hoo, hoo, hoo!

eat all the num-ber 'lev-en.

THINK IT THROUGH
Why do you think these three melodies sound good together?

THESE MELODIES REALLY GET AROUND!

Arthur Benjamin used the melody of "Mango Walk" and part of the countermelody of "Sweet Potatoes" in his composition "Jamaican Rumba."

LISTENING

Jamaican Rumba *by Arthur Benjamin*

LISTEN to a section of "Jamaican Rumba." Sing along with the orchestra when you hear a melody you know.

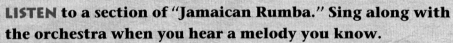

Theme 1

Theme 2

LISTENING MAP *Follow the listening map as you listen to*
"Jamaican Rumba."

MOVE with "Jamaican Rumba." Do the steps you know on
"Mango Walk" or create movements on the countermelody.

WORK RHYTHMS

Working to the rhythm of a song can make almost any task easier. "Zum gali gali" is a work song from Israel. The phrase *Zum gali gali* imitates the sound of a stringed instrument.

Zum gali gali

Israeli Work Song

A Ostinato

Em · Am · Em

Hebrew: זוּם גָּ - לִי, גָּ - לִי, גָּ - לִי, זוּם גָּ - לִי, גָּ - לִי.
Pronunciation: zum ga li ga li ga li zum ga li ga li
English: Zum ga - li, ga - li, ga - li, Zum ga - li, ga - li.

Em · Am · Em

זוּם גָּ - לִי, גָּ - לִי, גָּ - לִי, זוּם גָּ - לִי, גָּ - לִי.
zum ga li ga li ga li zum ga li ga li
Zum ga - li, ga - li, ga - li, Zum ga - li, ga - li.

B Verse

Em · Am · Em

הֶ - חָ - לוּץ לְ - מַעַן עֲ - בוֹ - דָה, –
he xa lutz lə man a vo da
Pi - o - neers work hard on the land,_____

80

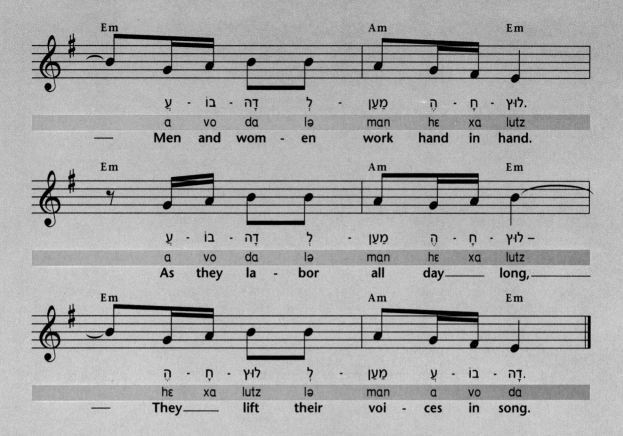

Em   Am   Em

עֲ - בוֹ - דָה לְ - מַעַן הֶ - חָ - לוּץ.

a vo da lə man hɛ xa lutz

— Men and wom - en work hand in hand.

Em   Am   Em

עֲ - בוֹ - דָה לְ - מַעַן הֶ - חָ - לוּץ –

a vo da lə man hɛ xa lutz

As they la - bor all day‗‗‗ long,‗‗‗

Em   Am   Em

הֶ - חָ - לוּץ לְ - מַעַן עֲ - בוֹ - דָה.

hɛ xa lutz lə man a vo da

— They‗‗‗ lift their voi - ces in song.

The sixteenth notes in "Zum gali gali" give it a driving rhythm.
Since four **sixteenth notes** equal one quarter note (♫♫ = ♩),
many of these notes can fit in each $\frac{2}{4}$ measure. Rhythm patterns
such as ♫♪ or ♪♫ can be made by combining sixteenth
notes and eighth notes. Which combination of notes is used in
"Zum gali gali"?

Name the songs that have the rhythm patterns below.

PLAY AN ACCOMPANIMENT

"The Rhythm of Life" shares the same driving rhythmic energy as "Zum gali gali." You can add even more energy with a rhythmic accompaniment.

PLAY these patterns as an accompaniment to "The Rhythm of Life." Start by playing A once with its repeat, B once with its repeat, and C once with its repeat. Then play all three patterns at the same time until the end.

A Claves or Clap

B Drum or Desk top

C Tambourine or Speak

Brr   rum bum bum bum   Brrr   rum bum bum bum

CREATE a new pattern to play with the A or B section. Choose a new percussion sound to perform the new pattern.

RHYTHM WORKOUT

Here's a chance to put what you've learned about
rhythm into action.

READ the rhythms below silently.

IDENTIFY the song from which each rhythm comes and
match each pattern with one of the pictures.

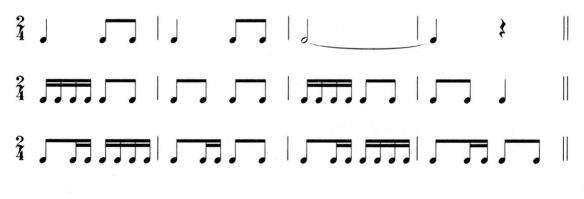

FASCINATING MELODIES

Look at the melody below. The pitches are here, but where is the rhythm? It's in your memory!

Read and sing these pitches to yourself. The order of the pitches will be so familiar that you'll probably fill in the missing rhythm as you sing and play.

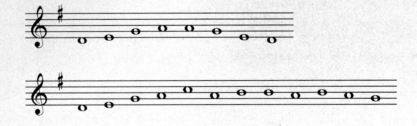

PLAY the melody on resonator bells.

Have you guessed the song yet?

MOVE with your hands to show each pitch.

FOLLOW the pictures to do a "hand dance" of the pitches in the melody.

Compose a different ending for the A section of "I Got Rhythm." Play or sing the pitches Gershwin used for the words *I got rhythm, I got music, I got my friends.* Create a new ending by choosing a different order for the pitches, still ending on G, the tonal center. Here are some possibilities.

PLAY or sing your new melody, and then trade melodies with a classmate. Do you think Gershwin might have experimented in this way?

Spotlight on the GERSHWIN BROTHERS

When the Gershwin brothers, George and Ira, started out in the songwriting business back in the 1920s, ragtime was the rage in St. Louis, and Dixieland jazz was taking over in New Orleans. George Gershwin understood how to shape an easy-to-remember melody with toe-tapping rhythms.

LISTENING

I Got Rhythm (piano version)
by George Gershwin

A **variation** in music occurs when a composer makes changes. Variations are enjoyable because you can recognize what you know and at the same time be surprised by something new.

LISTENING MAP Listen and follow the map as André Watts plays George Gershwin's piano variations on "I Got Rhythm." It should be easy because you are familiar with the form.

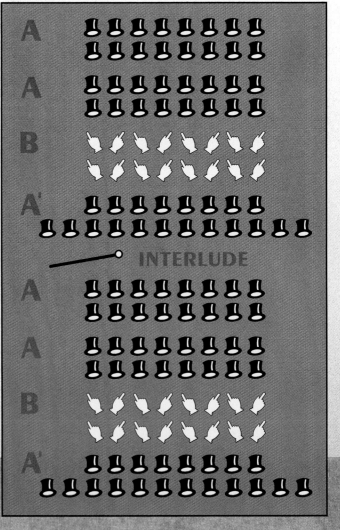

Both George and Ira grew up in New York City. Ira was quiet and shy and loved to read books. George, however, was mischievous and always looking for adventure. When the Gershwin family bought a secondhand piano, it was intended for the older son, Ira, but George was far more interested. He couldn't seem to get enough music. Ira became a writer, and often wrote lyrics for George's songs. "Fascinating Rhythm" is from **Lady, Be Good**, a musical that was a smash hit in both New York and London.

Fred Astaire with
George and Ira Gershwin

Fascinating Rhythm from *Lady, Be Good*

by George Gershwin and Ira Gershwin

IDENTIFY the pitches
by their letter names.

A **motive** is a small building block of melody or rhythm. The first six notes of "Fascinating Rhythm" make up a motive. By starting the motive on a different beat each time, Gershwin changed where the stresses fall as the motive is repeated.

"Fas - ci - nat - ing Rhy-thm, You've got me on the go! Fas - ci -

nat - ing Rhy - thm, I'm all a - qui - ver."

TAP lightly on the dashes as you listen to this section of "Fascinating Rhythm," and then repeat and sing as you tap.

A *Latin American* EXPERIENCE

Colombia
SOUTH AMERICA

Imagine the sound of a bass drum, then cowbells ringing out. As you run towards the plaza, the rhythm of the conga drum joins in. You see a blur of whiteness and light as dancers shuffle and swirl with candles held high.

On the Atlantic coast of Colombia, the *cumbia* dance is performed at night, with candles providing the only light. The woman dances with shuffling steps and the man moves in a zigzag pattern around her. The music for the *cumbia* is the most popular kind of folk song in that region.

LA CUMBIA

Popular Colombian Dance

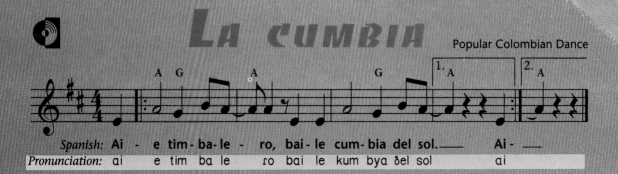

Spanish: **Ai - e tim - ba - le - ro, bai - le cum - bia del sol.____ Ai -**
Pronunciation: ai e tim ba le ɾo bai le kum bya ðel sol ai

88

"La cumbia" wouldn't be the same without drums and cowbells. The percussion accompaniment, so important in this music, is created by changing note values and stresses. However, that doesn't explain all of the rhythmic interest in "La cumbia." There is another element that creates the sound: instrumental tone color. You can make differences in tone color with body percussion.

PAT in different ways: with flat hands, with cupped hands, switching from one leg to the other or from the side of your leg to the top.

PAT the following pattern using different hand combinations.

Here's one way the pattern can be written.

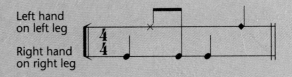

Left hand
on left leg

Right hand
on right leg

PLAY the pattern from notation. Be sure to make a difference in the tone color.

✕ means a closed sound, patting with a flat hand

◆ means an open sound, patting with a cupped hand

PLAY the pattern again as some of your classmates sing "La cumbia."

"La cumbia" has percussion parts for a conga drum, two cowbells, and bass drum. Each instrument makes more than one sound.

TRY these sounds. If you don't have an instrument, use substitute instruments or body percussion.

Conga drum—open (ringing) sound

Hit edge of drumhead with fingers. Let hand bounce.

Conga drum—closed (muffled) sound

Hit middle of drumhead with hand flat.

Strike side of drum with stick for a different sound.

Cowbell—open sound

Hold cowbell up. Keep index finger away from cowbell.

Hit side of cowbell with stick. Let it ring.

Cowbell—closed sound

Hit side of cowbell with stick while holding index finger against side of cowbell.

Bass drum—open sound

Strike drumhead with mallet. Let it ring.

Bass drum—closed sound

Hold free hand flat on drumhead and strike drumhead with mallet.

Play these parts with "La cumbia." In the score below, ♩ means to play with an open sound. ♩̸ means to play with a closed sound.

Play the top line of the conga part with the left hand. Play the bottom line of the conga part with a stick on the side of the drum.

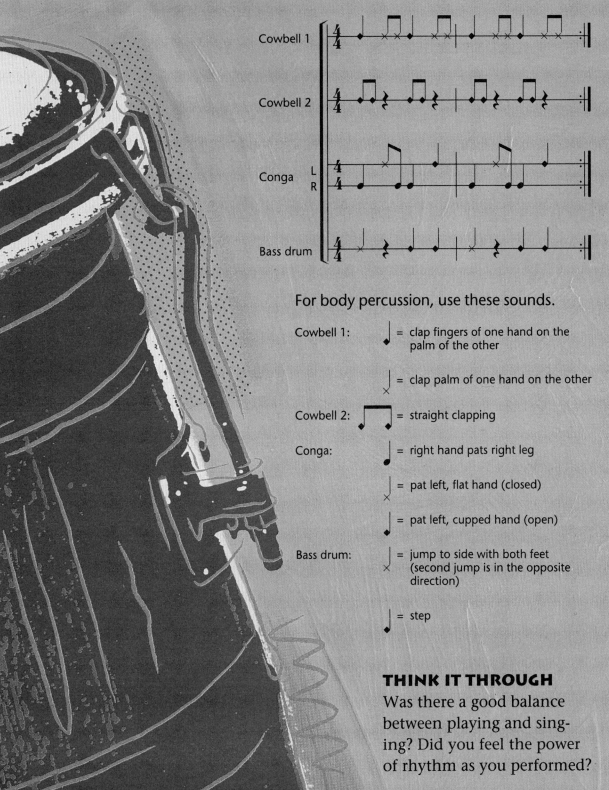

For body percussion, use these sounds.

Cowbell 1:   ♩ = clap fingers of one hand on the palm of the other

              ♩̸ = clap palm of one hand on the other

Cowbell 2:   ♫ = straight clapping

Conga: ♩ = right hand pats right leg

              ♩̸ = pat left, flat hand (closed)

              ♩ = pat left, cupped hand (open)

Bass drum: ♩̸ = jump to side with both feet (second jump is in the opposite direction)

              ♩ = step

THINK IT THROUGH
Was there a good balance between playing and singing? Did you feel the power of rhythm as you performed?

RHYTHM IN THE AIR

Where there's music, there's rhythm. Rhythmic characteristics of music can vary widely, depending on where it was created.

Think about differences in the cultures of western Africa and Taiwan. Cultural differences as well as differences in subject matter can affect music and the way that rhythm is treated.

Sing "Funga Alafia" and "Gau Shan Ching" and compare their moods. Notice how the African welcome song is syncopated and the Taiwanese mountain song has a more flowing rhythm.

The rhythm pattern ♪ ♩ ♪ that gives "Funga Alafia" its syncopation appears in music all over the world. It is a rhythmic motive in the Jamaican song "Mango Walk" and "This Train," a spiritual from the southern United States. Sing "Mango Walk" and "This Train" and clap the syncopated patterns.

Singing two different melodies at the same time can create a new rhythm not present in either of the separate songs. Sing "Sweet Potatoes" with its countermelody and notice the rhythmic "jigsaw puzzle" that results as these two pieces fit together.

If two melodies sung together can create rhythmic interest, think of the even more interesting combination of triple partner songs: "Mango Walk," "Sweet Potatoes," and the countermelody. Sing the triple partner songs "Sing for Your Supper."

Arthur Benjamin based his composition "Jamaican Rumba" on themes from "Mango Walk" and the countermelody of "Sweet Potatoes."

DANCE to "Jamaican Rumba." Add the rhythm of your movement to the rhythms of the orchestra.

CHECK IT OUT

1. Which rhythm do you hear?

   a.

   b.

   c.

   d.

2. Which rhythm do you hear?

   a.

   b.

   c.

   d.

3. Which rhythm do you hear?

   a.

   b.

   c.

   d.

4. Choose the pitches that you hear.

   a.

   b.

   c.

   d.

CREATE

Create Percussion Music

Compose a piece of music with two contrasting sections. Work with a partner. Create two different four-measure patterns in $\frac{4}{4}$ meter. Use ♩. ♪ and ♪ ♩ ♪ in one or both patterns.

COMPOSE a melody for each pattern using C D E F G. Begin on C or G. End on C.

CHOOSE a pitched percussion instrument to play each section.

PERFORM your composition.

Write

Arthur Benjamin used "Mango Walk" as part of a composition for orchestra. If you were going to write a composition for orchestra based on a song, what song would you choose? Write a brief paragraph describing your planned composition.

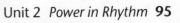

ENCORE

Messages in SOUND

In the music of Africa, percussion instruments are widely used. Drumming is especially important for communication and for celebration. The master drummer holds an honored position in society.

LISTEN to William Amoaku, a master drummer, talk about his art.

Proverbs, wise sayings that are passed down from generation to generation, are important in many cultures. The proverbs below are from the western part of Africa.

Learn well! Learn well!

One falsehood spoils the truth.

Little is better than nothing.

A dog's bark is not might but fright.

Children are rewards, (yes I say) children are rewards.

The teeth are smiling, but is the heart?

William Amoaku, master drummer

PRACTICE the rhythm of these proverbs. Use body percussion.

Like the master drummer, the griot plays an important role in traditional African culture. The griot, an expert in music, poetry, and story telling, travels from place to place sharing information among various communities. Griots, with their extensive memories and skill in narration, are important in helping to transmit the cultural heritage of the African people.

AFRICA
West Africa
Kenya

Selina Akua
Ahoklui,
a griot from
Ghana

PRACTICE the rhythm of the proverbs on percussion instruments. Then plan a performance with other class members that uses percussion instruments, movement, and speech.

THE FIERCE CREATURE
A FOLKTALE FROM KENYA

"The Fierce Creature" is a story told by the Masai people, who live in the high country of Kenya in eastern Africa. The story might be told by a griot at an outdoor gathering where the sounds of percussion and chirping insects can be heard.

The story tells of a tired caterpillar who, upon finding the empty home of a hare, sees a chance to take a nap. When the hare returns, he sees strange marks on the ground. He demands to know who is in his house. Afraid of being eaten, the cowardly caterpillar calls out in his fiercest voice. "I am the terrible warrior, deadlier than the leopard. I crush the rhinoceros to earth and trample the mighty elephant!" Hearing this, the hare hops up and down in fright.

A prowling leopard passes by, and the hare asks her for help. When the leopard calls out, asking who is there, the caterpillar repeats his warning. "I am the terrible warrior, deadlier than the leopard. I crush the rhinoceros to earth and trample the mighty

elephant!" This so frightens the leopard that she hides behind the hare.

A cranky rhinoceros comes next. Then a huge elephant thunders by. Each is asked for help. But after hearing the voice of the "warrior," they quake with fear and hide behind the others.

Finally, a frog hops by. He answers the caterpillar's cry with a ferocious shout of his own. "I, the hideous leaper, have come. I am slimy, green, and full of great warts!" This time, the frightened caterpillar makes a run for it. The others, catching sight of the little insect they had thought to be a fierce creature, enjoy a good laugh. The clever frog, however, makes off for a tasty meal.

DRAMATIZE the folk tale. Set the scene using the percussion sounds from the proverbs on page 96. Then choose instruments to represent each character. Play the instruments to accompany different parts of the folk tale.

EXPRESSIONS OF FREED

The Sidewalk Racer
or On the Skateboard

Skimming
an asphalt sea
I swerve, I curve, I
sway; I speed to whirring
sound an inch above the
ground; I'm the sailor
and the sail, I'm the
driver and the wheel
I'm the one and only
single engine
human auto
mobile.

—Lillian Morrison

101

Sing Out For Freedom

In the musical *The Wiz*, Dorothy, the heroine, melts the Wicked Witch with a bucket of water. Then everyone sings "Everybody Rejoice."

LISTEN to "Everybody Rejoice," and describe the differences in the voices you hear.

EVERYBODY REJOICE

Words and Music by Luther Vandross

1. Ev'-ry-bod-y look a-round, 'cause there's a rea-son to___ re-joice,___
2. Ev'-ry-bod-y be glad,___ be-cause the sun is shin-ing just___

___ you see.___ Ev'-ry-bod-y come out, and let's com-
___ for us.___ Ev'-ry-bod-y wake up, in-to the

mence to sing-ing joy-ful-ly.___ Ev'-ry-bod-y look up
morn-ing in-to hap-pi-ness.___ Hel-lo, world!

102

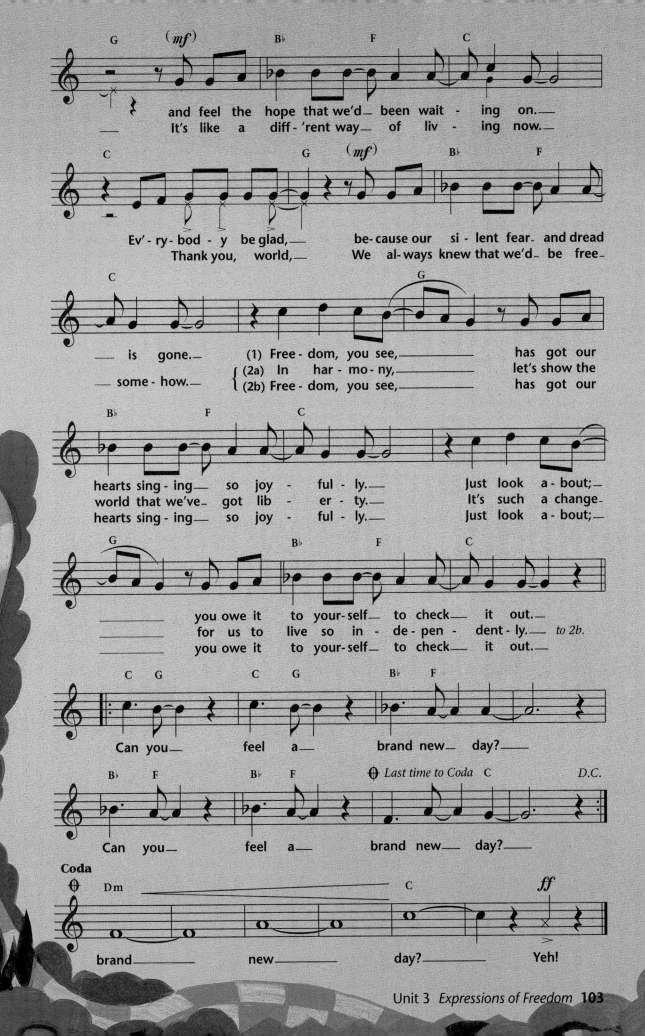

THE CHANGING SINGING VOICE

As you grow into an adult, your voice will become richer in quality and different in range. Your **unchanged** voice will become a **changed** adult voice.

Adult singing voices, both male and female, develop over a period of several years. They are usually classified according to their tone color and ranges. Below are the ranges of the four basic changed voices: **soprano, alto, tenor,** and **bass.**

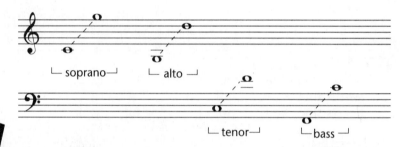

Unchanged voices share the same vocal range as the soprano and alto changed voices. The tenor and bass voices are lower. A singer with a tenor or bass voice often reads from the **bass clef** $\left(\text{𝄢} \right)$.

LISTENING

Lift Every Voice and Sing

by James Weldon Johnson and J. Rosamond Johnson

"Lift Every Voice and Sing" was written by two brothers. J. Rosamond Johnson composed the music and James Weldon Johnson wrote the **lyrics** (words). They wrote the song in 1900 to honor the late Abraham Lincoln. Lincoln was President during the Civil War and had ended slavery in the United States.

James Weldon Johnson later helped to found the National Association for the Advancement of Colored People (NAACP). "Lift Every Voice and Sing" is the NAACP's official song.

LISTEN to "Lift Every Voice and Sing." Decide if you hear changed voices or unchanged voices in this recording.

Along with freedom, people all over the world wish deeply for peace. The song "Shabat Shalom" uses a Hebrew phrase that expresses a wish for a peaceful Sabbath. The word *shalom* means "peace." It can be used as a greeting and a farewell.

FIND the measures with the syncopated pattern ♪ ♩ ♪

LISTEN to "Shabat Shalom" and decide if you hear changed or unchanged voices.

The modified grapevine step is part of a dance done with "Shabat Shalom."

Shabat Shalom

Words and Music
by N. Frankel

THINK IT THROUGH

You have been hearing and singing music that expresses everyone's need for freedom. How do you think music can express freedom in ways that words alone cannot?

MUSICAL

"When the Saints Go Marching In" was one of the first songs to be played in what was, in the early 1900s, a new and daring style of music called **Dixieland jazz.** Dixieland jazz started with small bands that played in New Orleans. These bands would begin with traditional spirituals and would freely experiment, or improvise, with the melodies to give them a completely new sound. Watch for the pitch between *mi* and *so* as you learn "When the Saints Go Marching In."

FREEDOM

When the Saints Go Marching In

African American Spiritual

1. Oh, when the saints _____ go march-ing in, _____
2. Oh, when the stars _____ re - fuse to shine, _____
3. Oh, when I hear _____ that trum - pet sound, _____

Oh, when the saints go march - ing in,
Oh, when the stars re - fuse to shine,
Oh, when I hear that trum - pet sound,

Oh, Lord, I want to be in that num - ber _____
Oh, Lord, I want to be in that num - ber _____
Oh, Lord, I want to be in that num - ber _____

When the saints go march - ing in.
When the stars re - fuse to shine.
When I hear that trum - pet sound.

BEYOND PENTATONIC—A NEW PITCH!

What are the letter names of the first four notes of "When the Saints Go Marching In"?

How many times do these pitches appear at the beginning of the song?

G is *do.* What are the pitch syllable names for B and D?

When G is *do,* the pitch syllable name for C is *fa.* You have sung and played this pitch many times. Now you can name it and read it on the staff.

G	B	C	D
do	*mi*	*fa*	*so*

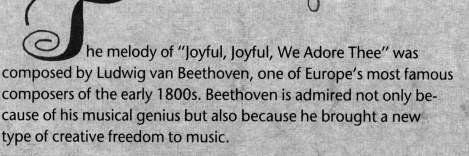

The melody of "Joyful, Joyful, We Adore Thee" was composed by Ludwig van Beethoven, one of Europe's most famous composers of the early 1800s. Beethoven is admired not only because of his musical genius but also because he brought a new type of creative freedom to music.

Henry van Dyke, an American, wrote English words to be sung to Beethoven's melody. "Joyful, Joyful, We Adore Thee" is the best known of van Dyke's hymns. It was first published in 1911.

Beethoven's manuscript
for Sonata No. 30 in
E Major, Op. 109

Joyful, Joyful We Adore Thee

Music Arranged from Ludwig van Beethoven
Words by Henry van Dyke
Words Adapted by Judy Bond

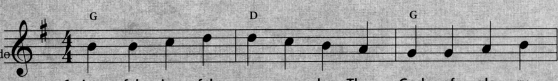

1. Joy - ful, joy - ful, we a - dore Thee, God of glo - ry,
2. All Thy works with joy sur - round Thee; Earth and heaven re -
3. Mor - tals join the might - y chor - us, Which the morn - ing

God of love, Hearts un - fold like flowers be - fore Thee,
flect Thy rays, Stars and an - gels sing a - round Thee,
stars be - gan. All cre - a - tion joins to - geth - er,

Open - ing to the sun a - bove. Melt the clouds of
Cen - ter of un - bro - ken praise. Field and for - est,
Son and daugh - ter, wom - an, man. Ev - er sing - ing,

sin and sad - ness, Drive the dark of doubt a - way.
vale and moun - tain, Flow' - ring mead - ow, flash - ing sea.
march we on - ward, Vic - tors in the midst of strife.

Giv - er of im - mor - tal glad - ness, Fill us with the light of day.
Chant-ing bird and flow - ing foun - tain, Call us to re - joice in Thee.
Joy - ful mu - sic lifts us sun - ward, In the tri - umph song of life.

SPOTLIGHT ON

Ludwig van
BEETHOVEN

Ludwig van Beethoven was born in 1770 and lived until 1827. He began composing music when he was only 11. He was a skilled pianist and often performed his piano music in public.

Beethoven's career influenced the lives and music of future composers. Up to that time, most musicians were treated like servants. Wealthy people hired composers to write music for special occasions.

During Beethoven's lifetime, public concerts were performed more often. Music publishing was growing into a profit-making industry. These developments helped composers earn money from works they had written. Beethoven had a strong personality. He insisted on writing music for his own satisfaction. The changing times, his abilities, and his fame allowed him to work almost independently of the wealthy.

Beethoven wrote music of all types, including nine symphonies. When he was at the height of his fame, he began to lose his hearing. In spite of this, he continued to compose and perform. By the end of his life, he was unable to hear at all. When Symphony No. 9 was first performed, Beethoven conducted, but he could not hear the applause. One of the musicians had to turn him around so that he could see the outpouring of enthusiasm from the audience. Because of Beethoven's great creativity and his courage, he is considered both a great composer and an inspiration to all who have to work in the face of difficulties.

🎵 Symphony No. 9

LISTENING

🔊 in D Minor, Op. 125 ("Choral"),
Fourth Movement (excerpt)

by Ludwig van Beethoven

*A **symphony** is a musical work. It is usually composed for instruments. During Beethoven's lifetime, the symphony was a very popular form. Beethoven was always looking for ways to make his music more powerful. In his last symphony, he added voices to the sound of the orchestra. The chorus sings part of a poem by Friedrich Schiller called "Ode to Joy." The words and music combine to create an exciting feeling of rejoicing and celebration.*

This symphony was performed at a special concert in Germany in 1989. In that year, the Berlin Wall was taken apart. For nearly 30 years the wall had divided the city of Berlin into East and West zones. The destruction of the wall was a symbol of liberty and unity for the German people and the world. For this concert, American conductor Leonard Bernstein had the original word for "joy" in German changed to the word that means "freedom."

LISTEN for a melody you know in Symphony No. 9.

Brandenburg Gate and
the Berlin Wall

TONE COLORS
of Orchestral Percussion

Percussion instruments play an important part in an orchestra. In the picture below are some of the percussion instruments Beethoven used in his Symphony No. 9. Can you name them?

mallets

drumhead

MEET THE TIMPANI

There are two types of percussion instruments: unpitched and pitched. Snare drums and maracas are two examples of those that do not sound a definite pitch. Xylophones and timpani are examples of those that can sound exact pitches.

Timpani (also called **kettledrums**) are usually played in sets of two or more. The player strikes the drums with large padded mallets. Each drum is tuned to a different pitch. The drum consists of a bowl-shaped copper base, across which is stretched a skin or plastic drumhead. The drumhead is held in place by a metal ring.

pedal

A player can change the pitch of each drum by adjusting the tension of the drumhead either by turning large screws around the rim of the drumhead or by raising or lowering a pedal attached to the drumhead by rods.

Timpani are known for their ability to produce loud rolls (rapidly repeating notes), which can be heard over the entire orchestra. Timpani also make the **bass line** (low notes) stronger by playing selected notes.

LISTEN again to Symphony No. 9 by Beethoven. Decide whether the timpani are playing rolls or playing selected notes.

Galerie Louis Carré et Cie., Paris

ORCHESTRE À LA PIANISTE, 1941

Raoul Dufy made many sketches and paintings of orchestras. The figures are general shapes, not finely detailed. Where are the timpani in this painting? What other orchestral instruments can you identify?

Fanfare for the Common Man

by Aaron Copland

A **fanfare** is a short, showy tune for trumpets or brass, played to honor important people or to announce an important event. Aaron Copland wrote "Fanfare for the Common Man" to express his concern for each individual's right to live in freedom and dignity. This piece honors every man and woman.

LISTENING MAP   Listen for the brass and percussion instruments as you follow the listening map.

Instruments play the theme in a "Follow the Leader" style.

THINK IT THROUGH

If you were to write music to honor someone, whom would you choose? Why?

SEVEN
STEPS TO MELODY

The melody for "Song of Peace" was written in 1899 by Jean Sibelius, Finland's most famous composer. The words to "Song of Peace" were written by Lloyd Stone. They speak of the special love one has for a homeland and express a wish for world peace.

LISTEN to the recording of "Song of Peace." It is sung *a cappella,* or without instrumental accompaniment.

DECIDE if you hear changed or unchanged voices in "Song of Peace."

118

Song of PEACE

Music by Jean Sibelius
Words by Lloyd Stone
Words Adapted by Judy Bond

1. This is my song, a song for all the na-tions,
2. My coun-try's skies are blu-er than the o-cean,

A song of peace for lands a-far and mine.
And sun-light beams in clo-ver leaf and pine.

This is my home, the coun-try where my heart is,
But oth-er lands have sun-light, too, and clo-ver,

Here are my hopes, my dreams, my ho-ly shrine;
And skies are ev'-ry-where as blue as mine.

But oth-er hearts in oth-er lands are beat-ing
O hear my song, a song for all the na-tions,

With hopes and dreams as true and high as mine.
A song of peace for their land and for mine.

A JOKE BACKFIRES

There is a lot of mystery about when "Yankee Doodle" was written and who wrote it. The tune is very old and came from Europe. Many sets of words have been used with this melody.

One story of the song's origin tells that new words were written by a British officer in 1755 to make fun of the colonial soldiers in America. The colonial soldiers, instead of being offended by the words, liked them. The song became one of the most popular songs during the time of the American Revolution.

YANKEE DOODLE

Traditional Melody
Words by Dr. Richard Shuckburgh
Descant by Mary Goetze

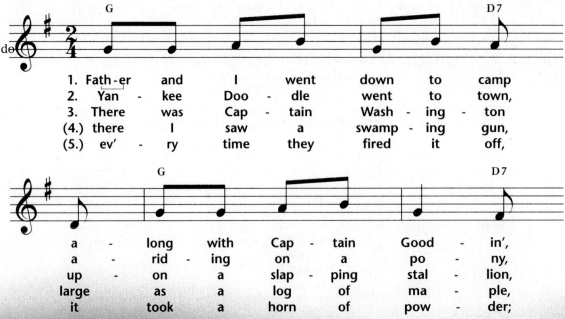

G   D 7

1. Fath-er and I went down to camp
2. Yan - kee Doo - dle went to town,
3. There was Cap - tain Wash - ing - ton
(4.) there I saw a swamp - ing gun,
(5.) ev' - ry time they fired it off,

G   D 7

a - long with Cap - tain Good - in',
a - rid - ing on a po - ny,
up - on a slap - ping stal - lion,
large as a log of ma - ple,
it took a horn of pow - der;

and there we saw the men and boys
He stuck a feath-er in his cap
a- giv-ing or-ders to his men;
up- on a might-y lit-tle cart;
it made a noise like Fath-er's gun

as thick as hast-y pud-din'.
and called it mac-a-ron-i.
I guess there were a mil-lion.
a load for Fath-er's cat-tle.
on-ly a na-tion loud-er.

Refrain

Descant

Step with the mu-sic and step with the band.

Melody

Yan-kee Doo-dle keep it up, Yan-kee Doo-dle dan-dy,

Step with the mu-sic, it's Yan-kee Doo-dle dan-dy.

Mind the mu-sic and the step, and with the girls be han-dy.

4. And
5. And

6. And there I saw a little keg,
   Its head all made of leather,
   They knocked upon't with little sticks
   To call the folks together.
   Refrain

7. I can't tell you half I saw,
   They kept up such a smother;
   I took my hat off, made a bow,
   And scampered home to Mother.
   Refrain

ONE LAST PITCH!

With one more pitch, you will know
all the tones of the major scale.

**LOOK at part of "Yankee Doodle" written below.
Figure out the syllables you know. Stop when you
come to a pitch that is a new one to you.**

The new pitch leads us "home" to *do*. This pitch is between
la and *do*. *Ti* is the name of this new pitch syllable.

THE DIATONIC SCALE

The pitches in a **diatonic scale** include all the pitches you have
learned: *do re mi fa so la ti do*'. A diatonic scale with *do* as the
tonal center is called a **major scale.** All of the songs in this lesson
use the major scale.

**NAME the syllables for "Ev'rybody Loves Saturday
Night" when G is *do*.**

EV'RYBODY LOVES SATURDAY NIGHT

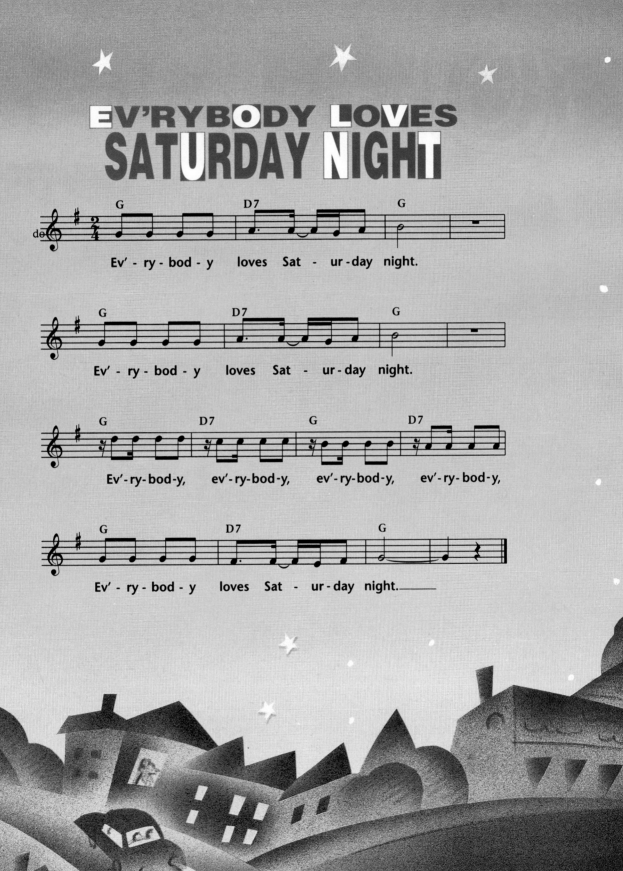

STEPS TO A NEW SOUND

Paris Opera House stairway

You have learned that a diatonic scale with *do* as its tonal center is a major scale. The word *scale* comes from the Italian word *scala,* which means "stairway."

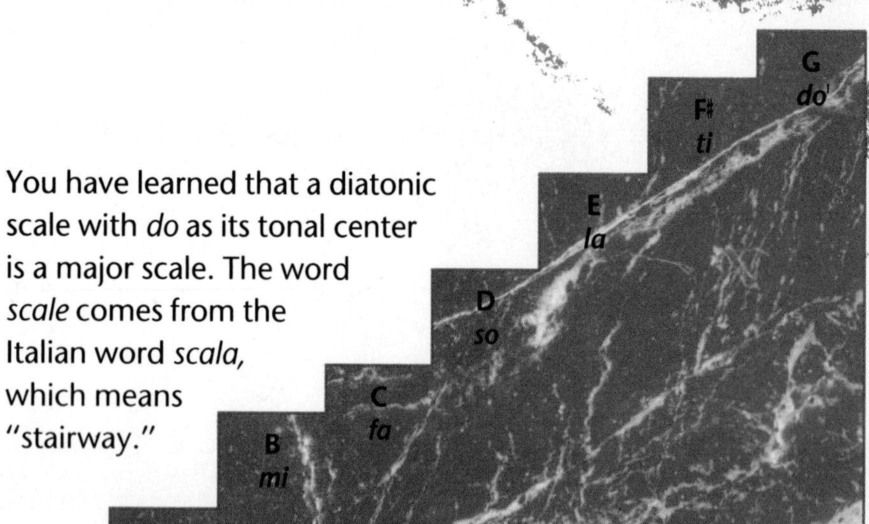

G
do¹

F#
ti

E
la

D
so

C
fa

B
mi

A
re

G
do

G
la

F
so

E♭
fa

D
mi

C
re

B♭
do

A
ti

G
la

When the tonal center is changed to *la,* the scale sounds different and has a different name. A diatonic scale with *la* as its tonal center is called a **minor scale.**

RELATIVITY

Relativity is an optical illusion by M. C. Escher. Follow the flights of steps and notice what happens to them. Floors turn into walls and walls become floors.

"Harriet Tubman" is a song about an American who played an important role in history. She helped about 300 enslaved people escape to freedom in the mid-1800s by a route known as the Underground Railroad.

DECIDE if "Harriet Tubman" is in major or minor.

The Granger Collection

Moderate, With Rhythmic Drive

Words and Music by Walter Robinson

1. One night I dreamed— I was in slav - ery,
2. Hun - dreds of miles— we trav - elled on - ward,

'bout eigh - teen fif - ty was— the time;—
gath - er - ing slaves— from town— to town.

Sor - row was the on - ly sign,—
Seek - ing ev' - ry lost— and found,

noth - ing a - round— to ease— my mind.
set - ting those free— that once— were bound.—

Out of the night— ap - peared a la - dy
Some - how my heart— was grow - ing weak - er,

lead - ing a dis - tant pil - grim band.____
fell by the way - side's sink - ing sand.____

"First mate," she called, point - ing her hand,____
Firm - ly did this la - dy stand,____

"make room a - board____ for this____ young wom - an,"
lift - ed me up____ and took____ my hand.____

Refrain
Say - ing, "Come on up." uh__ huh "I've got a life - line,

Come on up to this train____ of mine. Come on up," uh__ huh

"I've got a life - line, Come on up to this train____ of mine."____

Strongly
She said her name was Har - ri - et Tub - man,

and she drove____ for the Un - der - ground__ Rail - road.____

Expressio

Music is a powerful way to express emotions and ideas. Movement can provide yet another way to express both words and music.

EXPRESS the drama of "Harriet Tubman" with gestures.

1. One night I dreamed

2. I was in slavery

5. nothing around to ease my mind.

6. Out of the night appeared a lady

128

3. 'bout eighteen fifty was the time;

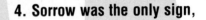

4. Sorrow was the only sign,

7. leading a distant pilgrim band.

8. "First mate," she called, pointing her hand, "make room aboard for this young woman."

This song was written in the 1960s. What events or situations
might have inspired Billy Taylor to write this song?

I Wish I Knew How It Would Feel
To Be Free

Music by Billy Taylor
Words by Billy Taylor and Dick Dallas

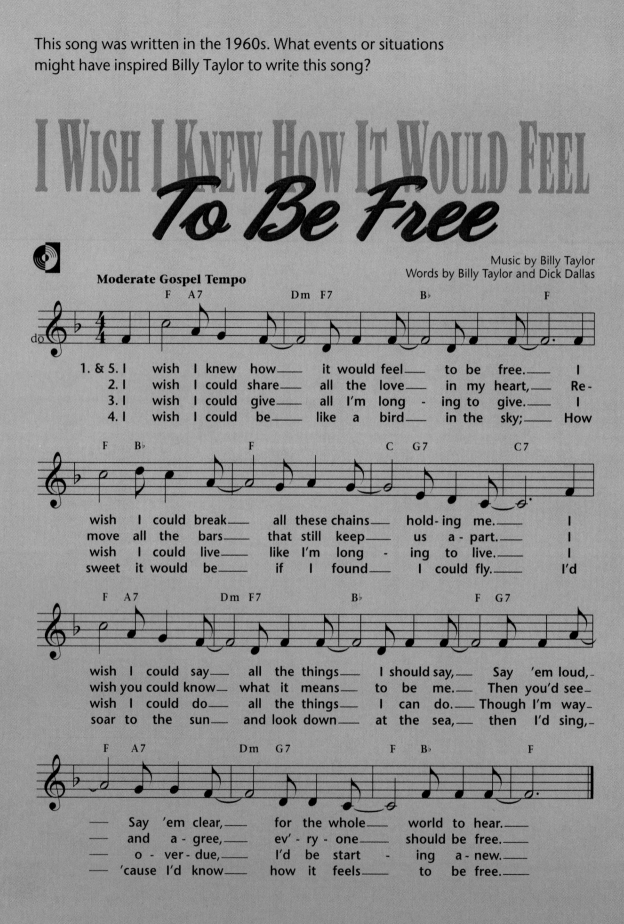

Moderate Gospel Tempo

| F   A7 | Dm   F7 | B♭ | F |

1. & 5. I wish I knew how—— it would feel—— to be free.—— I
2. I wish I could share—— all the love—— in my heart,—— Re-
3. I wish I could give—— all I'm long - ing to give.—— I
4. I wish I could be—— like a bird—— in the sky;—— How

| F   B♭ | F | C   G7 | C7 |

wish I could break—— all these chains—— hold-ing me.—— I
move all the bars—— that still keep—— us a-part.—— I
wish I could live—— like I'm long - ing to live.—— I
sweet it would be—— if I found—— I could fly.—— I'd

| F   A7 | Dm   F7 | B♭ | F   G7 |

wish I could say—— all the things—— I should say,—— Say 'em loud,-
wish you could know—— what it means—— to be me.—— Then you'd see-
wish I could do—— all the things—— I can do.—— Though I'm way-
soar to the sun—— and look down—— at the sea,—— then I'd sing,-

| F   A7 | Dm   G7 | F   B♭ | F |

—— Say 'em clear,—— for the whole—— world to hear.——
—— and a - gree,—— ev' - ry - one—— should be free.——
—— o - ver - due,—— I'd be start - ing a - new.——
—— 'cause I'd know—— how it feels—— to be free.——

Evans-Tibbs Collection, Washington, D.C.

ASPIRATION

Aspiration, the title of Aaron Douglas's painting, means "a desire to reach a goal." What goals do you think the people in the painting are moving toward?

THINK IT THROUGH

If you wrote a song about freedom today, what freedoms would you write about?

Billy Taylor

FINLAND'S FREEDOM

SPOTLIGHT ON JEAN SIBELIUS

The melody for "Song of Peace" was written by Jean Sibelius (1865-1957), Finland's most famous composer. It wasn't until he was 15 that Sibelius began to take a serious interest in music. When he finally began his musical studies, he quickly became a very good violin player and even tried composing. When he was 20, he was sent to Helsinki to study law. Within the year, he decided that music was what he really wanted as his life's work.

Sibelius studied music in Berlin and Vienna for several years. When he returned to Finland in 1891, his love for his homeland led him to compose a piece for orchestra based on Finnish subjects. A work for orchestra that tells a story through music is called a **tone poem.**

Sibelius's music was so highly valued in Finland that when he was 32 years old, his government awarded him a yearly amount of money so that he could spend all of his time composing.

LISTENING

Finlandia
Op. 26, No. 7 (excerpt)
by Jean Sibelius

Finland is a small country, one of the farthest north in Europe. It has often been involved in struggles for its freedom. When Sibelius was growing up, Finland was ruled by Russia. Sibelius was one of many Finnish people who worked for independence from Russia.

Sibelius's music inspired the Finnish people. His famous tone poem Finlandia, *written in 1899, became the anthem for the Finnish independence movement. The Russian government would not allow it to be performed. In 1917, Finland finally gained its independence from Russia and* Finlandia *could be heard again.*

Ateneum, Helsinki/The Central Art Archives

THE FIGHTING CAPERCAILLIES

The Fighting Capercaillies by Ferdinand von Wright is a favorite painting in Finland. It shows a scene in a Finnish forest. It is early morning and the mist is rising above a lake and bog. Can you find the third bird?

LISTEN to *Finlandia*. **What qualities of this music might inspire you to love your country? Which parts of the music suggest a struggle? When do you hear the sound of hope for freedom?**

LISTENING MAP *Follow this listening map with* **Finlandia.**

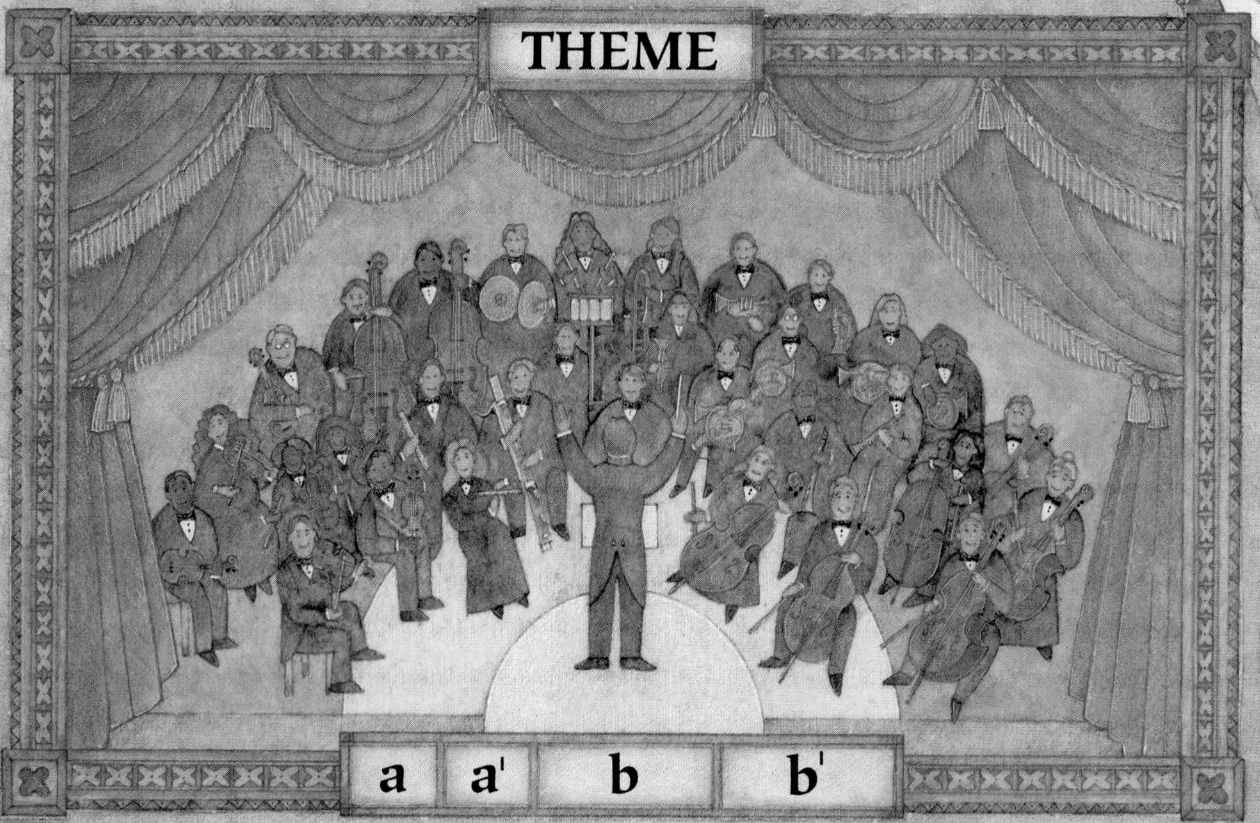

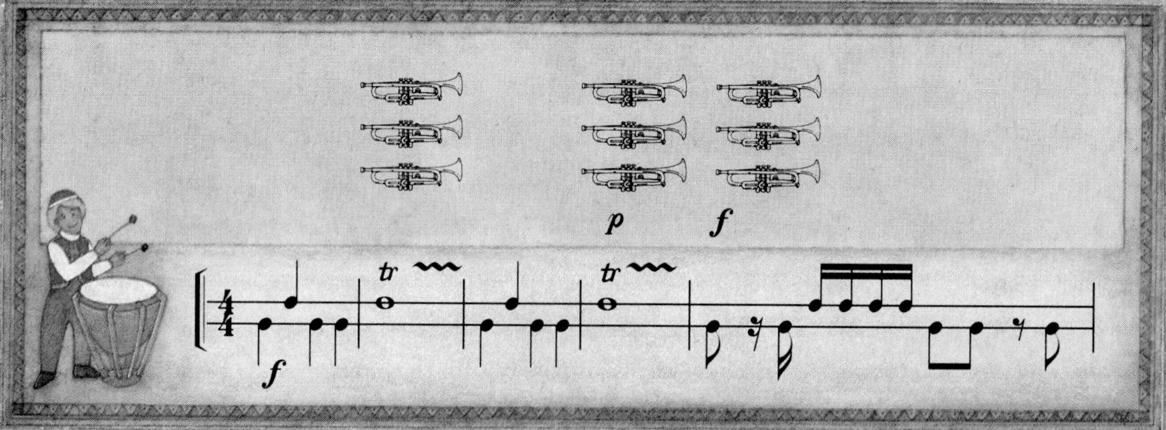

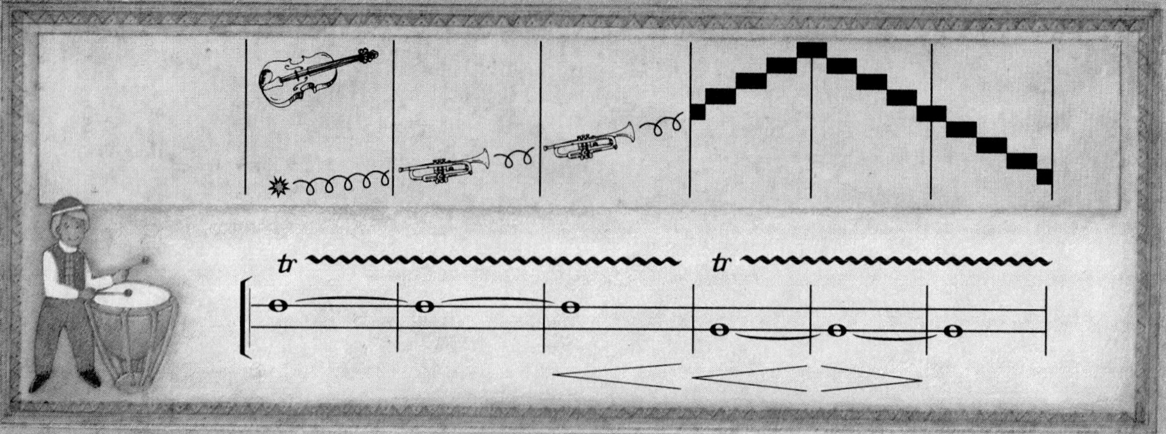

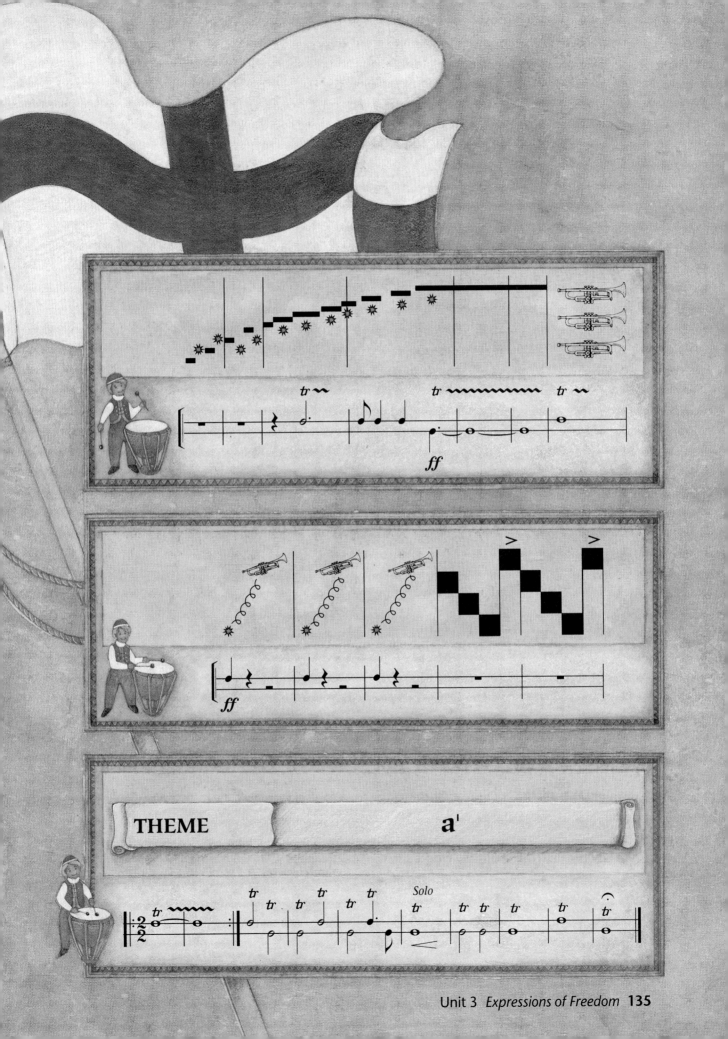

LOOKING TOWARD FREEDOM

LISTENING

N'kosi Sikelel' i Afrika
by Enoch Sontonga (additional sections by SEK Mqhayi and others)

Africans brought by force to the United States by slave traders were not the only people who were not free. People from many parts of the world have suffered at the hands of other people. Black people in South Africa have lived under unfair authority of white people for many years.

In 1897, Enoch Sontonga composed "N'kosi Sikelel' i Afrika," also known as "Prayer for Africa." This song captured the hearts of black Africans. Soon schoolchildren and popular singing groups were singing this song in many parts of Africa.

The African National Congress adopted it as a closing anthem for its meetings. It is accepted today by many black Africans as their national anthem.

FOLLOW the words as you listen to
"N'kosi Sikelel' i Afrika."

ZULU	ENGLISH
N'kosi sikelel' i Afrika,	Bless, oh Lord, our country Africa,
Maluphakanyisw' uphondo lwayo;	So that all may see her glory held high;
Yizwa imithandazo yethu.	Listen and protect us, be our guide.
N'kosi sikelela, N'kosi sikelela.	God bless, God bless.
(N'kosi sikelela, Thina lusapho lwayo.)	God bless, we her children.
Woza moya, Woza moya,	Spirit descend, Spirit descend,
Woza moya, oyingcwele.	Spirit descend, Spirit divine.
N'kosi sikelela, Thina lusapho lwayo.	God bless, we her children.

Think about how you treat others. How is the person in the poem being treated?

from
Equality

You declare you see me dimly
through a glass which will not shine,
though I stand before you boldly,
trim in rank and marking time.

You do own to hear me faintly
as a whisper out of range,
while my drums beat out the message
and the rhythms never change.

Equality, and I will be free.
Equality, and I will be free.

—Maya Angelou

Above: Capetown, South Africa *Right:* Masai women singing *Borders:* Designs from Ndebele walls, Transvaal, South Africa

La golondrina by *Francisco Serradell*

In Mexico, a symbol of freedom is the swallow, la golondrina. This song often reminds people of their homeland. The singer feels like the homesick swallow but hasn't the freedom to fly back home as the bird does.

Think of your favorite memories of home as you listen to "La golondrina." What would you choose for a symbol of your hometown?

Many African American spirituals speak of going to heaven. For those who were enslaved, heaven was a symbol of a happy home where all would be free. "When the Saints Go Marching In" expresses this joyous view of heaven.

SING "When the Saints Go Marching In"
with "This Train" as partner songs.

Moving On

When the Saints Go Marching In

African American Spirituals

Oh, when the saints go march-ing

This Train

This train is bound for glo - ry,

in, Oh, when the saints go march - ing

this train, This train is bound for glo - ry,

in, Oh, Lord, I want to be in that

this train, This train is bound for glo - ry,

num- ber When the saints go march - ing in.

If you ride it, you must be ho - ly, This train is bound for glo- ry, this train.

SONGS OF FREEDOM

"Yankee Doodle" is more than just a silly song about a man with a feather in his cap. It was an important song in the American colonists' struggle to become free from England's rule. The British sang a version of it to make fun of the colonists' armies early in the Revolutionary War. The American patriots turned the song around and used it to unite themselves against the British. Sing this song and enjoy its catchy rhythms.

Freedom—could anyone doubt its importance to all of us? Enslaved people, torn from their homelands in Africa, knew how important freedom was. Many were willing to risk life itself to gain their freedom. Think about their journeys to freedom as you sing "Harriet Tubman." Listen to how the minor key helps to express the feeling of the words.

Joy can come with freedom. This joy is clearly expressed in the song "Everybody Rejoice." Sing "Everybody Rejoice" and notice that the major key supports the positive message of this song.

The hope of all is that peace will come with freedom. The melody of "Song of Peace" comes from the stirring tone poem *Finlandia* by Jean Sibelius, a work for orchestra that deals with love of country. Sing "Song of Peace" with the recording and listen to the soprano, alto, tenor, and bass voices as you sing.

People all over the world work in many ways for peace and freedom. Sing "Shabat Shalom," an Israeli song. The words mean "peaceful Sabbath."

CHECK IT OUT

1. What do you hear?

   a. changed   **b.** unchanged voices

2. What do you hear?

   a. changed   **b.** unchanged voices

3. What do you hear?

   a. changed   **b.** unchanged voices

4. Which of these is major?

   a. Example A   **b.** Example B   **c.** Example C

5. Which of these is minor?

   a. Example A   **b.** Example B   **c.** Example C

CREATE

Freedom Songs Interview

PLAN an interview on the topic of freedom songs. Work with a small group to develop questions for the interview and choose the person to be interviewed.

Tape the interview if possible. Record your subject's name, occupation, and national background. During the interview, ask your subject to sing a freedom song and tell something about the song.

PRESENT your findings to the class, using excerpts from the tape.

End your presentation by performing a freedom song selected by members of the group. Tell why the group chose the song.

Write

Which song or listening selection in this unit best agrees with your own idea of freedom? Write a letter to an imaginary friend sharing one of your ideas or opinions about freedom. Include a description of the music you chose and explain to your friend why this fits your idea of freedom.

HARRIET,
the Woman Called
MOSES

"This Train" and "Swing Low, Sweet Chariot" are African American spirituals that express the longing of enslaved Africans for freedom. One person who led many Africans to freedom was Harriet Tubman. Born in slavery in Maryland around 1820, she escaped to freedom in 1849. Soon afterwards, she worked with the Underground Railroad. This was a network of antislavery people in the United States that helped slaves to escape. At the risk of her own life, Tubman led more than 300 slaves to the North and to Canada.

LISTEN closely to the words of "Go Down, Moses."

GO DOWN, MOSES

African-American Spiritual

Freely

Solo Gm   D   Gm   *Group* D   Gm

When   Is - rael   was in   E - gypt's land,   Let   my   peo - ple   go!
No   more   shall   they in   bond - age   toil,   Let   my   peo - ple   go!

Solo Gm   D   Gm   *Group*   D   Gm

Op - pressed   so   hard they could not   stand,   Let   my   peo - ple   go!
Let   them   come out   with   E - gypt's spoil,   Let   my   peo - ple   go!

Gm   Cm   Gm

Go down,   Mo - ses,   'way   down   in   E - gypt's land.—

Gm   D   Gm

Tell   old   Phar - oah,   to   Let   my   peo - ple   go!

The composer Thea Musgrave was inspired by the story of Harriet Tubman. She decided to write an opera about this courageous person. The opera is based on Tubman's life. By weaving spirituals such as "Go Down, Moses" and "Swing Low, Sweet Chariot" into the music, Musgrave established the atmosphere for the opera.

A scene from the opera *Harriet, the Woman Called Moses.*

🎵 Harriet, the Woman

🔵 Called Moses (excerpts)

by Thea Musgrave

LISTEN to a section from the beginning of the opera.

Harriet, now free, is dreaming about her youth, when enslaved people were forbidden to sing spirituals. As she begins to sing "Go Down, Moses," her brother Benji begins to sing and play the drums. Notice how the composer combines her melodies and harmonies with the spiritual melody.

Why do you think the enslaved Africans were not allowed to sing "Go Down, Moses?"

A successful opera production combines the talents of many people—costume designers, stage set designers, musicians, conductors, and music coaches. The most important part, however, is the singing.

In an opera, there are usually several main characters with different types of voices.

COMPARE the vocal qualities of the singers as you listen.

Harriet mourns the death of her friend Josiah.

A special challenge for the composer of an opera is to give the singers magnificent music to show off their voices. Other challenges are to develop each character and to keep the story moving forward. This requires skill in writing a drama as well as in writing music. Often a composer will work with a **librettist,** a person who writes the **libretto,** or text, to an opera. Thea Musgrave, however, wrote both the music and the libretto for *Harriet, the Woman Called Moses.*

Meet THEA MUSGRAVE

Thea Musgrave was born in Scotland in 1928. As a child she always liked music. However, when she graduated from public school, she enrolled as a pre-medical student at the University of Edinburgh. After a brief period of pre-medical studies, Thea Musgrave knew she could not ignore her first love—music. Three years later, in 1950, she graduated with a music degree. Her decision was wise. Her compositions have received great praise for their dramatic quality and different styles. In addition to composing, Thea Musgrave has conducted a number of her own works. She has received many awards in recognition of her work.

LISTEN to Thea Musgrave talk about her experiences of composing *Harriet, the Woman Called Moses.*

SEA
TO
SHINING
SEA

from

I hear America singing,
   the varied carols I hear, . . .
Each singing what belongs to him
   or her and to none else, . . .
Singing with open mouths
   their strong melodious songs.

—Walt Whitman

149

TRAVELING THROUGH AME

In 1893 Katharine Lee Bates traveled to the top of Pikes Peak in Colorado. As she viewed "the purple mountain's majesty above the fruited plain," she was inspired to write the poem "America, the Beautiful." Later her words were added to a melody composed by Samuel Ward.

SING "America, the Beautiful" and imagine yourself looking at your country from a mountaintop or from space.

America, the Beautiful

Music by Samuel Ward
Words by Katharine Lee Bates

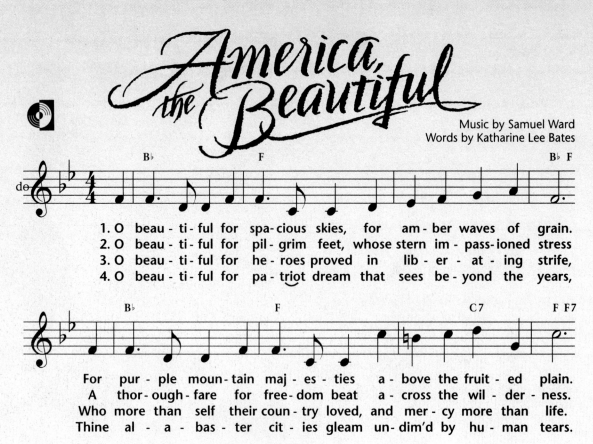

1. O beau - ti - ful for spa - cious skies, for am - ber waves of grain.
2. O beau - ti - ful for pil - grim feet, whose stern im - pass-ioned stress
3. O beau - ti - ful for he - roes proved in lib - er - at - ing strife,
4. O beau - ti - ful for pa - triot dream that sees be - yond the years,

For pur - ple moun - tain maj - es - ties a - bove the fruit - ed plain.
A thor - ough - fare for free - dom beat a - cross the wil - der - ness.
Who more than self their coun - try loved, and mer - cy more than life.
Thine al - a - bas - ter cit - ies gleam un - dim'd by hu - man tears.

A - mer - i - ca! A - mer - i - ca! God shed His grace on thee,
A - mer - i - ca! A - mer - i - ca! God mend thine ev' - ry flaw,
A - mer - i - ca! A - mer - i - ca! May God thy gold re - fine,
A - mer - i - ca! A - mer - i - ca! God shed His grace on thee,

And crown thy good with broth- er- hood, from sea to shin- ing sea.
Con - firm thy soul in self - con - trol, Thy lib- er - ty in law.
Till all suc - cess be no - ble- ness, and ev'- ry gain di - vine.
And crown thy good with broth- er- hood, from sea to shin- ing sea.

THE UPS AND DOWNS OF METER

FIND the meter signature in "America, the Beautiful."

Different meters have different patterns of stressed and un-stressed beats. In $\frac{4}{4}$ meter, there is a pattern of one strong beat followed by three weak beats. Bar lines show where these patterns begin and end.

Music can begin with an **upbeat,** or incomplete measure. The upbeat includes one or more notes that occur on a weak beat. The upbeat leads to the **downbeat,** or strong beat. An upbeat can occur in several places in a song. A phrase may start on an upbeat or a downbeat.

FIND each upbeat in "America, the Beautiful."

You may have traveled by bicycle, car, truck, bus, or plane, but have you traveled by song? Many songwriters have made this kind of "travel" possible. In his song "Something to Sing About," Oscar Brand refers to favorite places throughout the United States.

Something to Sing About

Words and Music by Oscar Brand

C **F**

1. I have wan-dered my way through the won-ders of New York Bay,
2. I have wel-comed the dawn to the high-land of Or-e-gon,

C **Dm** **G7**

North to Ni - ag - 'ra to hear the falls roar,
Seen the moon light up the soft south-ern dew,

C **F**

Seen the waves tear in vain at the rock-cov-ered coast of Maine,
Where the sweet eve-ning breeze kissed the leaves of the lem-on trees,

C **G7** **C**

Watched them roll back from the New Eng-land shore.
Whis-p'ring the song that I'm shar-ing with you.

Refrain **G7** **C**

From the fair Ha-wai-ian is-lands to the Rock-y Moun-tain high-lands,

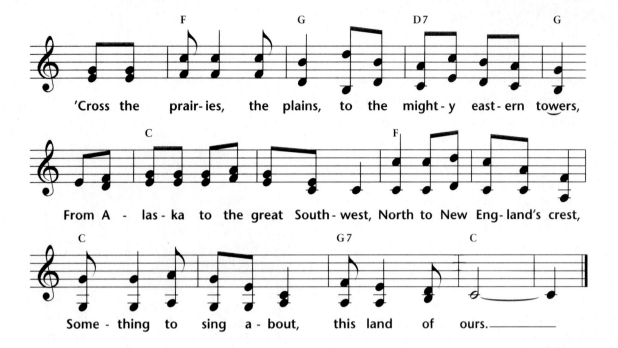

'Cross the prair-ies, the plains, to the might-y east-ern towers,

From A - las - ka to the great South - west, North to New Eng-land's crest,

Some - thing to sing a - bout, this land of ours._____

3. Yes, we've something to sing about, tune up a string about,
   Call out the chorus, or quietly hum,
   Of a land that's still young, with a ballad that's still unsung,
   Telling the promise of great things to come.

FIND the meter signature and tell what it means. How many phrases start with an upbeat?

THINK IT THROUGH

Have you been to any of the places mentioned in "Something to Sing About"? What places would you include if you wrote a song about your country?

WRITE your own verse for "Something to Sing About."

How would you like to travel by barge? The Erie Canal was built in the early 1800s to transport people and goods between Albany and Buffalo, New York. The canal linked the Hudson River with the Great Lakes. In those days, flat-bottomed boats called barges were towed by mules who walked beside the canal. "Erie Canal" is a song the mule drivers sang.

A **fermata** (⌒) means that the note or rest under it should be held longer than its normal value. Pause on that note or rest before going on.

View on a Canal, 19th-century woodcut

FIND the fermatas in "Erie Canal."

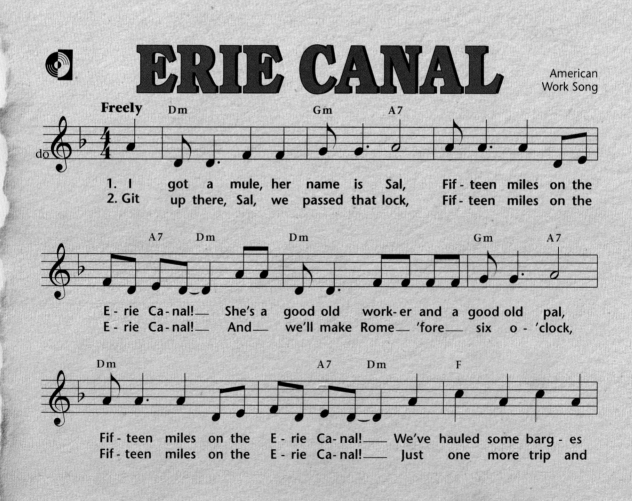

ERIE CANAL
American Work Song

Freely

1. I got a mule, her name is Sal, Fif - teen miles on the
2. Git up there, Sal, we passed that lock, Fif - teen miles on the

E - rie Ca - nal! She's a good old work-er and a good old pal,
E - rie Ca - nal! And we'll make Rome 'fore six o - 'clock,

Fif - teen miles on the E - rie Ca - nal! We've hauled some barg - es
Fif - teen miles on the E - rie Ca - nal! Just one more trip and

in our day,   Filled with lum-ber, coal and hay, And   we know ev'-ry
back we'll go, Through the rain and sleet and snow,'Cause we know ev'-ry

inch of the way From Al - ba - ny____ to____ Buf - fa - lo.____
inch of the way From Al - ba - ny____ to____ Buf - fa - lo.____

Refrain

Low bridge, ev'-ry-bod-y down, Low bridge, 'cause we're com-ing to a town;

And you'll al-ways know your neigh-bor, You'll al-ways know your pal,

If you ev-er nav-i-gat-ed on the E-rie Ca-nal.____

Junction of the Erie & Northern Canals by John William Hill

TRAVELING WITH MUSIC

A Sunday Excursion on the Ohio River, engraving, 1881

If you had lived during the last century, you might have traveled by steamboat or barge down the Ohio River from Pennsylvania all the way to Illinois. During your trip, you might have danced to a rollicking tune like "Down the River."

DOWN THE RIVER

American River Chantey

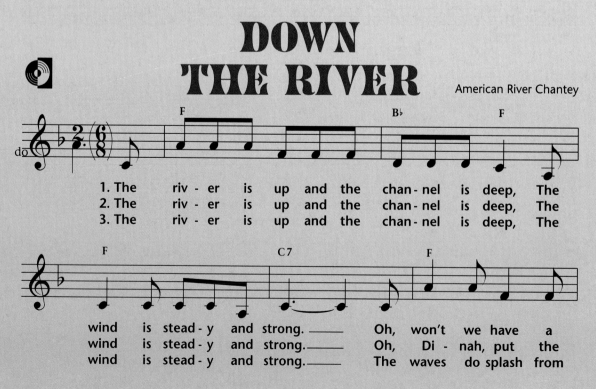

1. The riv-er is up and the chan-nel is deep, The
2. The riv-er is up and the chan-nel is deep, The
3. The riv-er is up and the chan-nel is deep, The

wind is stead-y and strong. Oh, won't we have a
wind is stead-y and strong. Oh, Di - nah, put the
wind is stead-y and strong. The waves do splash from

jol - ly good time, As we go sail - ing a - long.
hoe - cake on, As we go sail - ing a - long.
shore—— to shore, As we go sail - ing a - long.

Refrain
Descant
F   B♭
Melody
Down the riv - er, Oh, down the riv - er, Oh,

C7   F
down the riv - er we go.——

F   B♭
Down the riv - er, Oh, down the riv - er, Oh,

C7   F
down the O - hi - o!——

A **flat** (♭) placed on a note lowers its pitch a half step. A **half step** is the smallest distance between pitches in most music. A flat placed before a note is called an **accidental.** When a flat is placed at the beginning of each staff it is called a **key signature.** This means the flat is in effect throughout the piece of music.

FIND the flat in the key signature of "Down the River."

FOLLOW the pitches of the scale used in "Down the River" on the keyboard as you listen to the scale again.

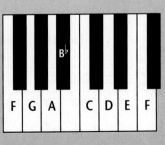

River travel may have been an important means of transportation in the past, but today people are more likely to travel by car or van. You can gather your friends or family, put on a cassette or CD, and you're ready to travel with music.

SING this country music by Willie Nelson.

On the Road Again

Words and
Music by Willie Nelson

1., 3. On the road a - gain._____ Just can't
(2.) road a - gain._____ Go - in'

wait to get on the road a - gain._____ The life I
pla - ces that I've nev - er been._____ See - in'

love is mak - ing mu - sic with my friends, and I can't wait to get
things that I may nev - er see a - gain, and I can't wait to get

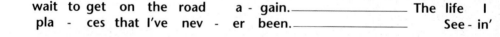

on the road__ a - gain._____ 2. On the
on the road__ a - gain._____

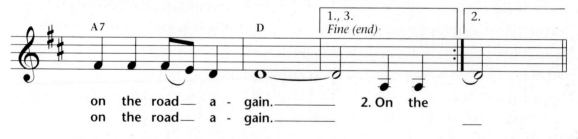

On the road a - gain,_____

On the road, Like a band of gyp - sies

We're the best of friends,___

we go down the high-way.___   On the

road, In - sist - ing that the world keep turn - ing our way,___

D.S. al Fine
(Go to % then to the End)

___ and our way,___ Is on the

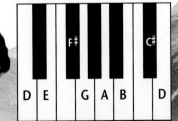

Just as the flat (♭) placed on a note lowers its pitch a half step, the **sharp** (♯) raises a pitch a half step. A sharp can be used as an accidental or in a key signature. The key signature of "On the Road Again" has two sharps. The key signature is a written reminder that sharps or flats are needed. A **natural** (♮) is used to cancel a sharp or flat.

FOLLOW the pitches on the keyboard below as you listen to the scale used in "On the Road Again."

MOVING ALONG BY STEPS

The major scale is made up of pitches that are a whole step or a half step apart. A half step is the smallest distance between pitches in most music. A **whole step** is twice that distance. Listen to the difference between a whole step and a half step.

Here are two melodic patterns from "Something to Sing About" that use pitches of the C major scale.

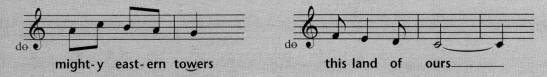

do   might-y east-ern towers

do   this land of ours_____

SING the melodic patterns with words, with pitch letter names, and with pitch syllables. Then sing the C major scale.

do

C   D   E   F   G   A   B   C
do re mi fa so la ti do'

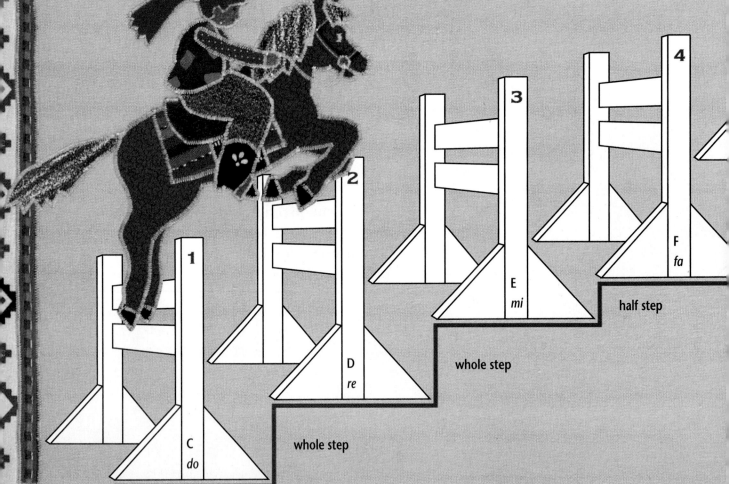

In the major scale, the half steps are between the third and fourth pitches and the seventh and eighth pitches. All the other steps are whole steps.

IDENTIFY the letter names of the pitches that are a whole step apart in the major scale below. Then identify the letter names of the pitches that are a half step apart.

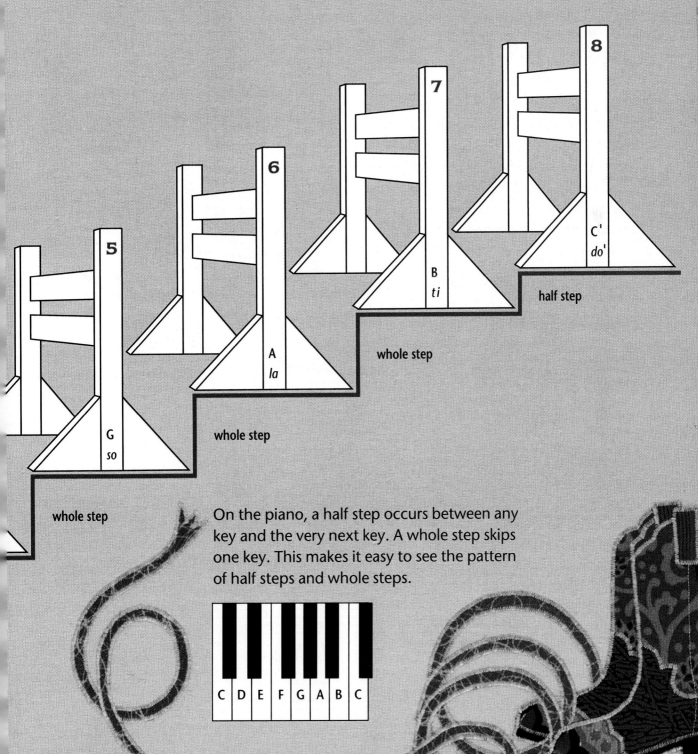

half step

whole step

whole step

whole step

On the piano, a half step occurs between any key and the very next key. A whole step skips one key. This makes it easy to see the pattern of half steps and whole steps.

MOVING THROUGH THE SOUTHLAND

The Ohio River joins the Mississippi River, which flows all the way to New Orleans. "Swing Low, Sweet Chariot" comes from the southern part of our country. It is in **verse-refrain** form. The words to the verse change. The refrain is the part of the song that stays the same.

Find the repeated words in "Swing Low, Sweet Chariot." These words are part of a style called **call and response.** The call is often a solo and the response is sung by a group. The response usually is a repeated phrase.

SWING LOW, SWEET CHARIOT

African American Spiritual

Refrain

Swing low, sweet char - i - ot,— Com-in' for to car-ry me home,

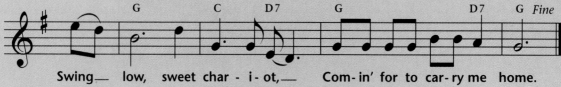

Swing— low, sweet char - i - ot,— Com- in' for to car-ry me home.

Verse

Leader   G   C   D7

1. I look'd o - ver Jor - dan an' what did I see,—
2. If you get there be - fore I do,—
3. I'm some - times up and some - times down,—

Group
G   D7   *Leader*   G

Com - in' for to car - ry me home, { A band of an - gels
                                Tell all my friends I'm
                                But still my soul feels

C   D7   *Group* G   D7   G *D.C. al Fine*

com - in' af - ter me,—
com - in' there too,— } Com - in' for to car - ry me home.
heav'n - ly bound,—

The phrase *comin' for to carry me home* is a repeated musical motive. Make an upward arc with your arm as a "movement motive"
on the words *comin' for to carry me home* in the refrain. Change
the way you do the movement each time by choosing a different
arm, level, or facing.

SING Verse 1 of "When the Saints Go Marching In"
as a partner song with the refrain of "Swing Low,
Sweet Chariot."

A MUSICAL MELTING POT

The Mississippi River flows south to Louisiana. There you might hear **zydeco,** a kind of dance music. Zydeco is a mixture of jazz and blues with Creole music, style, and language. "Et tan' patate là cuite" is in Creole, a language that has French roots.

The accordion, washboard, and fiddle were important in early zydeco music, but today the players may use saxophone, electric guitar, and drums also.

Zydeco band

LISTEN to the zydeco style in "Et tan' patate là cuite" and identify the instruments you hear and recognize.

Sing this traditional Creole song.

CREATE your own dance, following the form of the music.

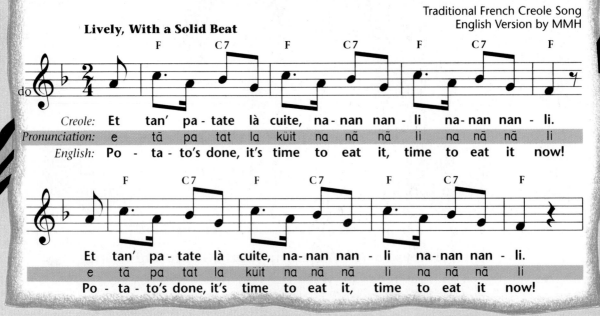

ET TAN' PATATE LÀ CUITE
POTATO'S DONE

Traditional French Creole Song
English Version by MMH

Lively, With a Solid Beat

Creole: Et tan' pa-tate là cuite, na-nan nan - li na-nan nan - li.
Pronunciation: e tã pa tat la küit na nã nã li na nã nã li
English: Po - ta-to's done, it's time to eat it, time to eat it now!

Et tan' pa-tate là cuite, na-nan nan - li na-nan nan - li.
e tã pa tat la küit na nã nã li na nã nã li
Po - ta-to's done, it's time to eat it, time to eat it now!

Even though "Et tan' patate là cuite" and "Swing Low, Sweet Chariot" are very different in style, they have something in common. Each song has two contrasting sections.

DESCRIBE the forms of "Swing Low, Sweet Chariot" and "Et tan' patate là cuite."

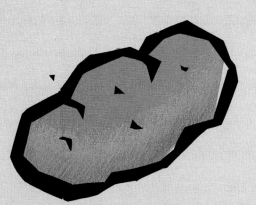

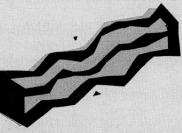

You Can't Go Far
WITHOUT METER

Traveling west from New Orleans, you would soon hit Texas. At one time, Texas belonged to Mexico. Some think the composer of "The Yellow Rose of Texas" was a volunteer in the Texan war for independence.

SING this famous Texas song and imagine the excitement you would feel if you re-turned to your home and family after being gone for a long time.

Music Adapted by Jay Arnold
Words Adapted by
Jay Arnold and Marilyn Davidson

The Yellow Rose of
TEXAS

1. There's a Yel-low Rose in Tex-as I'm go-ing home to see.
2. Where the Ri-o Grande is flow-ing, and stars are shin-ing bright,
3. Now I'm go-ing back to find her, my heart is full of woe.

I miss that lit-tle la-dy, I'm sure she miss-es me.
We walked a-long the riv-er one qui-et sum-mer night.
We'll sing the songs to-geth-er we sang so long a-go.

What is the meter signature of "The Yellow Rose of Texas"?

Explain what the meter signature tells you.

BE A METER READER

In $\frac{2}{4}$ ($\substack{2 \\ \circ}$) meter, the quarter note (♩) stands for one beat.
Each measure has two beats. The quarter note can be divided
into two eighth notes. ♩ = ♫ or ♪ ♪

In $\frac{6}{8}$ ($\substack{2 \\ \circ\cdot}$) meter, the dotted quarter note (♩.) lasts for one beat.
Each measure has two beats. The dotted quarter note can be
divided into three eighth notes. ♩. = ♫♪ or ♪♪♪
There are six eighth notes in a measure.

PERFORM rhythm patterns in $\frac{2}{4}$ and $\frac{6}{8}$.

In the 1800s, a railroad was built that went from coast to coast across the United States. Many immigrants from Europe and China helped to build this and other railroads. The photograph shows the celebration that took place at Promontory Point, Utah, when the railroad was completed.

SAY and clap these $\frac{6}{8}$ patterns. Find the same rhythm sequence in "Pat Works on the Railway."

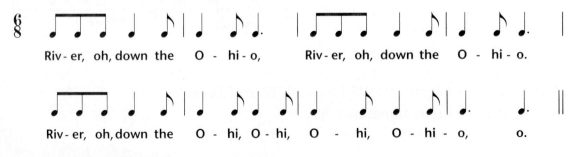

Riv- er, oh, down the   O - hi - o,   Riv- er, oh, down the   O - hi - o.

Riv- er, oh, down the   O - hi, O - hi,   O - hi, O - hi - o,   o.

This song is about one of the Irish railway workers.

PAT WORKS ON THE RAILWAY

American Railroad Song

1. In eigh - teen hun - dred and for - ty - one, I
2. In eigh - teen hun - dred and for - ty - two, I
3. In eigh - teen hun - dred and for - ty - three, 'twas
4. It's "Pat, do this,"___ and "Pat, do that," with -

put me cord - 'roy breech - es on, I put me cord - 'roy
left the old world for the new, 'Twas sor - ry luck that
then I met sweet Bid - dy Ma - gee, And an el - e - gant wife she's
out a stock - ing or cra - vat, And noth - ing but an

breech - es on to work up - on the rail - way.
brought me through to work up - on the rail - way.
been to me while work - in' on the rail - way.
old straw hat while work - in' on the rail - way.

Refrain

Fil - li - me - oo - re - i - re - ay, Fil - li - me - oo - re - i - re - ay,

Fil - li - me - oo - re - i - re - ay, To work up - on the rail - way.

Unit 4 *Sea to Shining Sea* **169**

WESTWARD BOUND ON A TRAIL OF music

Songs about America, work songs, songs for entertainment, and songs which express feelings—your musical journey has included all of these and more. Just as the world is filled with many different people, there are many different kinds of songs, each one with a special meaning for its time and place.

LISTEN to beginnings of songs you have learned and tell the name of each one. Find their locations on the map.

THINK IT THROUGH
"Erie Canal" and "Pat Works on the Railway" are both work songs. How are they alike? How are they different?

MIND YOUR MINOR

You probably realized the first time you heard "Pat Works on the Railway" that it has a minor sound. What makes music sound minor? It's because the melody is based on pitches in the minor scale and the tonal center is *la*. Just as you learned the arrangement of half steps and whole steps for the major scale, you can learn a different arrangement for the minor scale.

LISTEN to the E minor scale. Name the pitches that are a whole step apart, then the pitches that are a half step apart.

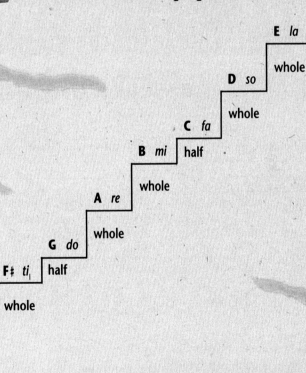

FOLLOW the pattern of half steps and whole steps on the piano keyboard.

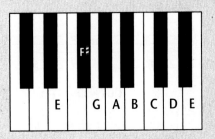

¡HOLA, AMIGO!

Throughout the Southwest, Spanish is often spoken and Spanish songs such as "Campanas vespertinas" are sung with beautiful harmony.

Before the wristwatch was invented, people often depended on the sound of church bells to tell the time of day. The sound of large bells can be heard from quite a distance.

LISTEN for the contrast between unison and two-part singing in this song about bells.

CAMPANAS VESPERTINAS
EVENING BELLS

Music by Julio Z. Guerra
Words by Juana Guglielmi
English Words by MMH

Spanish: Las cam - pa - nas de la i - gle - sia dan el to - que de o - ra - ción
Pronunciation: las kam pa nas de la i gle sya dan el to ke ðeo ɾa syon
English: Hear the ring - ing of the church- bells, hear them call - ing, hear the sound.

Y la luz del sol que mue - re a o-tro mun- do i - rá a-lum- brar.
i la lus ðel sol ke mwe ɾe ao tro mun doi ɾaa lum bɾar.
See the sun - light slow- ly dy - ing, as the eve - ning comes a -round.

¡Que dul - ce a - cen - to, ding, ding, ding, dong! Su voz a -
ke ðul sea sen to ding ding ding dong su ßos a
How sweet their ac - cent, Ding, ding, ding, dong! They lift my

le - gra mi co - ra - zón. ¡Ding ding ding dong!
le gra mi ko ɾa son ding ding ding dong
heart with their e - ven - song. Ding ding ding dong!

le - gra mi co - ra - zón. ¡Ding ding ding
le gra mi ko ɾa son ding ding ding
heart with their e - ven - song. Ding ding ding

Su voz a - le - gra mi co - ra - zón.
su βos a le gra mi ko ɾa son.
They lift my heart With their e - ven - song.

dong! Ay, mi co - ra - zón.
dong ai mi ko ɾa son.
dong! With their e - ven - song.

Taos Pueblo, New Mexico

A MUSICAL GAME FROM THE PLAINS

LISTENING

Eka Muda *Comanche Hand-Game Song*

Native Americans knew how beautiful this land was long before it was called America. The many Native American nations stretch "from sea to shining sea." Each has its own culture, language, and customs.

"Eka Muda" has been a popular hand-game song of the Comanches for many years. The game is played by people of all ages. In the Comanche language, eka muda means "You're no smarter than a red mule." The words are sung to tease members of the other team as the hand game is played.

LISTEN to "Eka Muda" as it is sung in the traditional style of the Plains Indians. Describe the vocal quality, mood, and instruments used in the accompaniment.

LISTEN to the song sung by students. Find the places where the voices slide up to the pitch (╱).

174

EKA MUDA

Comanche
Hand-Game Song

Comanche: E - ka mu - da,___ E - ka mu - da,___ He hai - ya
Pronunciation: e ka mu da e ka mu da he hai ya

E - ka mu - da, He hai - ya E - ka mu - da.
e ka mu da he hai ya e ka mu da

A COMANCHE VILLAGE

A Comanche Village shows Comanche
women curing buffalo hides. Buffalo
skins were used for many purposes,
including clothing and tepees, until the
buffalo became scarce. George Catlin,
the artist, spent several summers in the
1830s among various Indian groups.

Hide painted by Comanche women
Sioux beaded ball and doll

WHICH HAND?

The hand game for "Eka Muda" involves competition between two teams of players. For each round of play, one team chooses a "hider," the other team chooses a "guesser."

The hider holds two sticks, one in each hand. One stick has a special mark. As the song is sung by the hider's team, the hider moves his hands through the air and changes the sticks from hand to hand to confuse the guesser. When the hider brings his hands forward, the guesser tries to point to the hand that holds the marked stick.

If that hand has the marked stick, the guesser's team gets a counting stick. The teams change roles and the singing switches to the other team. If the hand with the marked stick was not selected, the hider's team gets a point and play continues without stopping the song.

Philbrook Museum of Art, Tulsa, Oklahoma

WINTER GAMES OF THE CHEYENNE

Winter Games of the Cheyenne by Dick West (Wah-pah-nah-yah) shows many Native American games. Find the people playing a stone-tossing game and "stick in the hoop." There is also wrestling, kickball, "snow snake" javelin throwing, tobogganing, and a game of "shinny."

"In New Mexico the land is made of many colors. When I was a boy I rode over the red and yellow and purple earth to the West Jemez Pueblo. My horse was a small red roan, fast and easy-riding. I rode among the dunes, along the bases of mesas and cliffs, into canyons and arroyos. I came to know that country, not in the way a traveler knows the landmarks he sees in the distance, but more truly and intimately, in every season, from a thousand points of view. I know the living motion of a horse and the sound of hooves. I know what it is, on a hot day in August or September, to ride into a bank of cold, fresh rain."

—from The Way to Rainy Mountain
by N. Scott Momaday, Kiowa

On the Trail

from *Grand Canyon Suite*
by Ferde Grofé

Just as Pikes Peak inspired Katharine Lee Bates to write the poem "America, the Beautiful," the Grand Canyon has inspired many others to create works of art, poetry, and music.

One composer who was inspired by the Grand Canyon was Ferde Grofé. Each movement of his Grand Canyon Suite tells a story: "Sunrise," "Painted Desert," "On the Trail," "Sunset," and "Cloudburst."

In "On the Trail," Grofé creates a musical image of the trip down into the canyon on the back of a mule. You can almost hear the sound of hooves on the stone and feel the rocking motion of the ride.

*This type of story-telling or image-making music is called **program music.** Can you name another example of program music that you heard earlier this year?*

GETTING TO THE

PAT the rhythm of Theme 1 in "On the Trail" with alternating hands.

Theme 1

To accompany Theme 1, Grofé used a steady "clip-clop" played on coconut shells. This part is written in **cut time** ($\mathrm{\mathbf{¢}}$ or $\frac{2}{2}$). In cut time, the half note gets one beat. There are two beats in a measure.

CLAP the clip-clop part with Theme 1 as you listen to these parts.

TRACE the melody of Theme 2 as you listen.

Theme 2

Listen for the two themes in "On the Trail" as you follow the map.

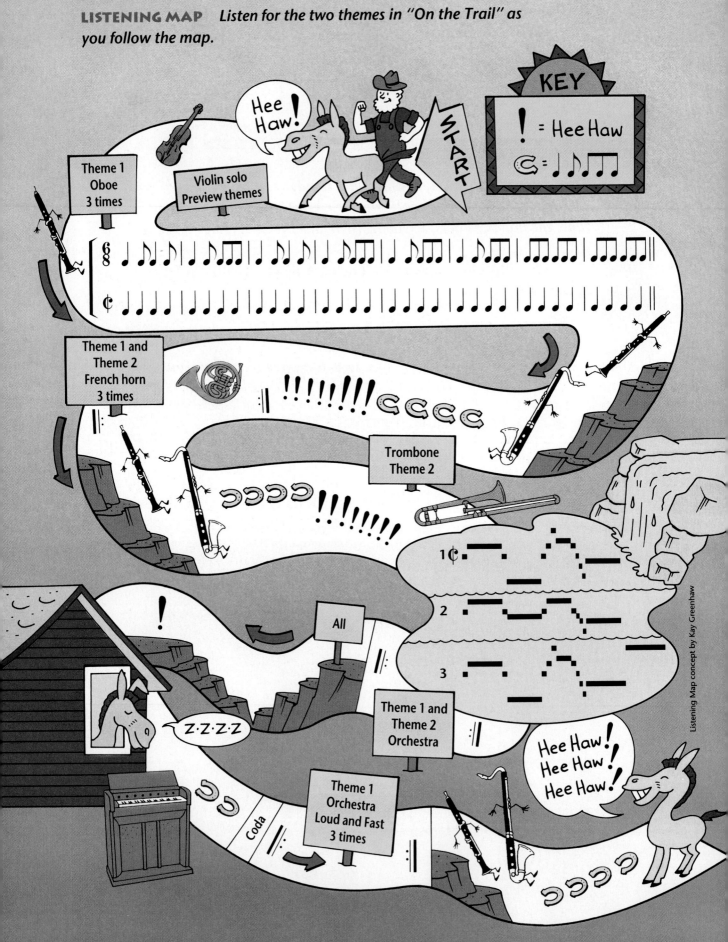

PUT YOUR SKILLS TO WORK

Clap the patterns below to check your reading skill.

CREATE an accompaniment for "Et tan' patate là cuite" or "Pat Works on the Railway" using rhythm patterns in $\frac{2}{4}$ or $\frac{6}{8}$. Work in a group to choose the song and create an eight-beat pattern in the meter of the song. How many patterns are needed to fit the form of the song?

CHOOSE percussion instruments and play your accompaniment as you sing the song.

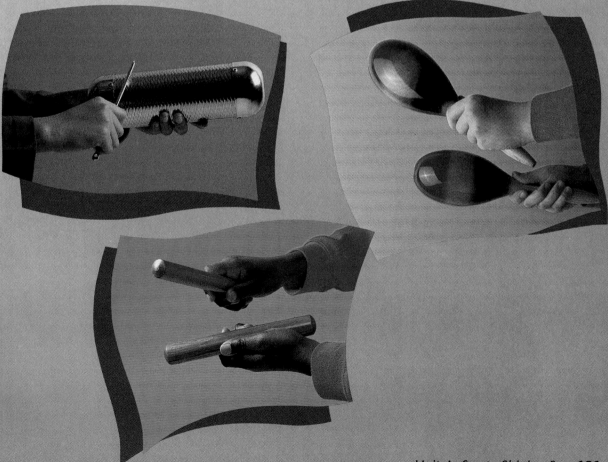

Journey's End

CONDUCT in 4/4 as you sing the first phrase of "This Train," "When the Saints Go Marching In," and "Swing Low, Sweet Chariot" separately. Conduct and sing the first phrases together. Then sing the three spirituals together as partner songs as you conduct.

Oh, when the saints

Swing low,

This train

California, here we come! Our destination is San Francisco, home of the Golden Gate Bridge. This city has inspired many songwriters.

San Francisco

Music by Bronislaw Kaper
and Walter Jurmann
Words by Gus Kahn

San Fran - cis - co, o - pen your gold - en gate.

You let no stran - ger wait out - side your door.

Oh, we throw the net out in-to the sea,___

and all the a-ma a-ma come a-swim-min' to me.___
a ma a ma

Oh, we're go-in' to the hu-ki-lau,
hu ki lau

hu - ki, hu - ki, hu - ki, hu - ki, hu - ki-lau.
hu ki hu ki hu ki hu ki hu ki lau

As I Row

*As I row over the plain
Of the sea and gaze
Into the distance, the waves
Merge with the bright sky.*

—Fujiwara No Tadamichi

San Fran - cis - co, here is your wan - dering one

Say - ing, "I'll wan - der no more."___

Oth - er plac - es on - ly make me love you best.

Tell me you're the heart of all the gold - en west.

2nd time ritard

San Fran - cis - co, wel - come me home___ a - gain.

2nd time molto rit.

I'm com - ing home___ to go roam - ing no more. more.___

FIND the meter signature in "San Francisco" and explain the meter to a friend.

CONDUCT in cut time as you sing "San Francisco."

1   2

Visit San Francisco

SAN FRANCISCO

ALOHA!

When Katharine Lee Bates wrote her famous poem "America, the Beautiful," our country was the land from the Atlantic Ocean to the Pacific Ocean—"from sea to shining sea." That changed in 1959, when Hawaii became our fiftieth state.

Your musical journey would not be complete without a song from Hawaii, where ocean fishing is popular. A *hukilau* is a fish feast. The people of a village catch a hundred or so fish in a huge circular net, then cook and eat them.

The Hukilau Song

Words and Music by
Jack Owens

Eng./Hawaiian: Oh, we're go - in' to the hu - ki - lau,
Pronunciation: hu ki lau

hu - ki, hu - ki, hu - ki, hu - ki, hu - ki, hu - ki - lau,
hu ki hu ki hu ki hu ki hu ki hu ki lau

Ev' - ry - bod - y loves the hu - ki - lau,
hu ki lau

where the lau - lau is the kau - kau at the hu - ki - lau.
lau lau kau kau hu ki lau

ACROSS THE COUNTRY IN SONG

The United States of America *from California to the New York island, from sea to shining sea*—this is a great land with great people. Sing "Something to Sing About" and recall all the places you sang about in Unit 4.

In the early days of the United States, the waterways were our lifelines. Sing "The Erie Canal," and imagine that you are making the long trip from Albany to Buffalo by barge.

Probably the most important river to the new nation was the Mississippi with its tributaries such as the Ohio. Boats of all shapes and sizes still go "Down the River."

Each state has its own history and traditions. When you travel across Texas, you can get a sense of how large our country is. Sing "The Yellow Rose of Texas" as you imagine traveling across Texas on horseback at the time this song was written.

People have come from all over the world to make new homes in the United States. In the mid-1800s, people came from Europe as well as from Asia to help build the Transcontinental Railway. Sing "Pat Works on the Railway," a song that tells the story of railway workers from Ireland.

The personality of different parts of the country comes from the people who lived there in the past as well as from the people who live there today. The Southwest has a Spanish flavor because the first Europeans who settled there were from Spain. Sing "Campanas vespertinas."

This vast land of ours, with its cities and towns, deserts, mountains, rivers and lakes, and its rich variety of people surely is "America, the Beautiful."

SING "On the Road Again" and "America, the Beautiful."

CHECK IT OUT

1. Choose the meter you hear.

   a. $\frac{4}{4}$ b. $\frac{6}{8}$

2. Which of the following examples shows what you hear?

3. Which of the following examples shows what you hear?

   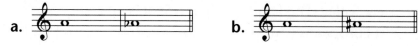

4. Choose the $\frac{6}{8}$ pattern you hear.

   a.   b.   c.   d.

5. Which pattern is in $\frac{6}{8}$ meter?

   a. Example A   b. Example B

6. Which pattern is in $\frac{6}{8}$ meter?

   a. Example A   b. Example B

7. Which pattern is in $\frac{6}{8}$ meter?

   a. Example A   b. Example B

CREATE

Plan and Perform a Program

Plan a program around the theme "Sea to Shining Sea." Review songs, dances, and poetry learned in this unit, and select some of them for performance. The beginning song should set the mood and the ending song should reinforce or sum up the theme.

Create a script from information in your book as well as additional research.

PRACTICE the program and then present it to an audience.

Write

Which place in the United States would you most like to visit? Write an essay or poem about this place. Tell what type of music you might hear in your chosen place.

Encore
SIMPLE GIFTS
The World of the Shakers

Look at the pictures on this page. What do they tell you about the people who created these objects?

The Shakers are a religious group, founded in this country in 1774. Their small communities were in northern New York state, New England, and the Midwest. The scenes on these pages show their fine crafts. Although today their population is very small, the Shaker way of life and the high quality of their crafts are still much admired.

DESCRIBE the kind of music you think Shakers might have created. Listen to the song. Were you correct?

SIMPLE GIFTS

Shaker Song

'Tis the gift to be sim - ple, 'tis the gift to be free,

'Tis the gift to come down where we ought to be.

And when we find our - selves in the place just right,

'Twill be in the val - ley of love and de - light.

When true sim - pli - ci - ty is gained,

To bow and to bend we shan't be a - shamed.

To turn, turn will be our de - light,

Till by turn - ing, turn - ing we come 'round right.

Variations on Simple Gifts
from Appalachian Spring
by Aaron Copland

Aaron Copland chose "Simple Gifts" to use in his music for the ballet Appalachian Spring. Even though the Shakers are not in his ballet, Copland felt that the song expressed the spirit of all early settlers. The ballet is about a pioneer celebration of a recently married couple at a newly built farmhouse in Pennsylvania.

LISTEN for the melody in its original form and in *augmentation*, a technique in which all of the note values are doubled.

LISTENING MAP As you listen to "Variations on Simple Gifts," follow the pictures that represent the variations. Each picture shows an everyday activity with friends and relatives helping out.

Theme   Variation 1   Variation 2   Variation 3

Variation 4   Coda

QUILTS
An American Folk Tradition

Most early American settlers made all of their own cloth. They wove the cloth themselves and dyed it with dyes made from flowers, leaves, or berries from their own gardens. From the cloth, they made bed linens, quilts, and clothing.

The quilts made by the early settlers were often beautifully designed. People still enjoy making quilts today. Square scraps of cloth are sewn together to form colorful patterns. The stitching itself is frequently done so well that it adds to the beauty of the quilt. Often, several friends will work together to make a quilt. The pleasure of their combined efforts adds to their satisfaction in accomplishment.

LOOK at the quilts below. In what way is making a quilt like creating a rhythm or melody pattern?

Expressions of Style

Music

Music is a tale told in sounds
Of such infinite reach
All time, all life, all tongues
Are in its speech.
Music is the sound of events
So moving, in its classic or its blue,
The heart nods recognition: "I was there.
And I have felt that, too . . ."

—Mary O'Neill

195

A Musical Style Show!

The many kinds of music reflect the ideas of the people who created them. Musical styles reflect the dreams and feelings of people from near and far, from the past and the present.

The elements of music are rhythm, pitch, harmony, texture, dynamics, tempo, and tone color. The distinct ways that people use these elements to express themselves create a **style** of music. The time, place, and purpose of the music also affect its style.

LISTENING

Pitched Percussion Montage

LISTEN to "Pitched Percussion Montage" and think about how to describe the different styles. Follow the pictures as you listen. How are the instruments alike or different? Which instruments are familiar?

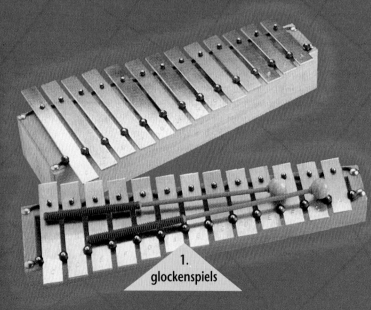

3.
angklung

2.
cloud
chamber bowl

1.
glockenspiels

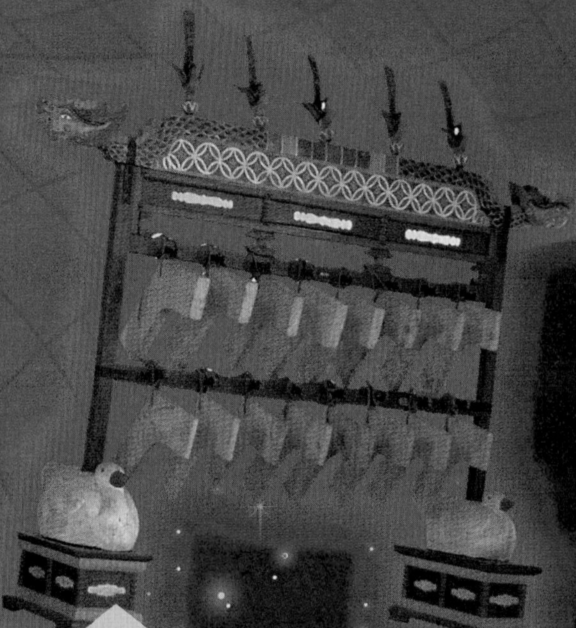

4.
stone chimes

5.
steel drum

AMERICAN POPULAR STYLE

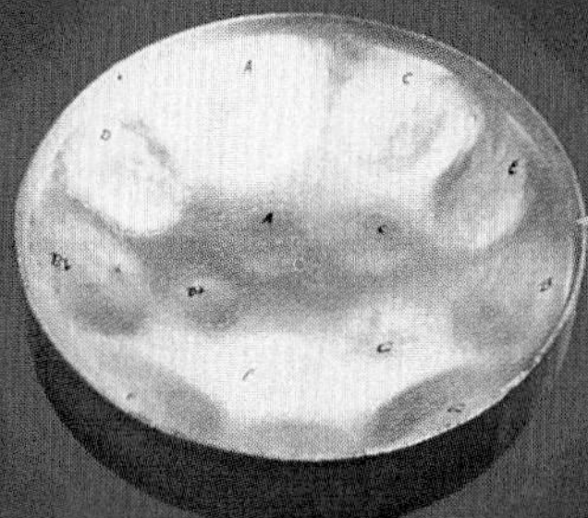

"Music! Music!" is in a style you've heard before. It is in an American popular song style.

DESCRIBE the musical elements as they are used in this song. What do you think makes it sound like a popular song?

MUSIC! MUSIC!

Words and Music by
Frederick Silver

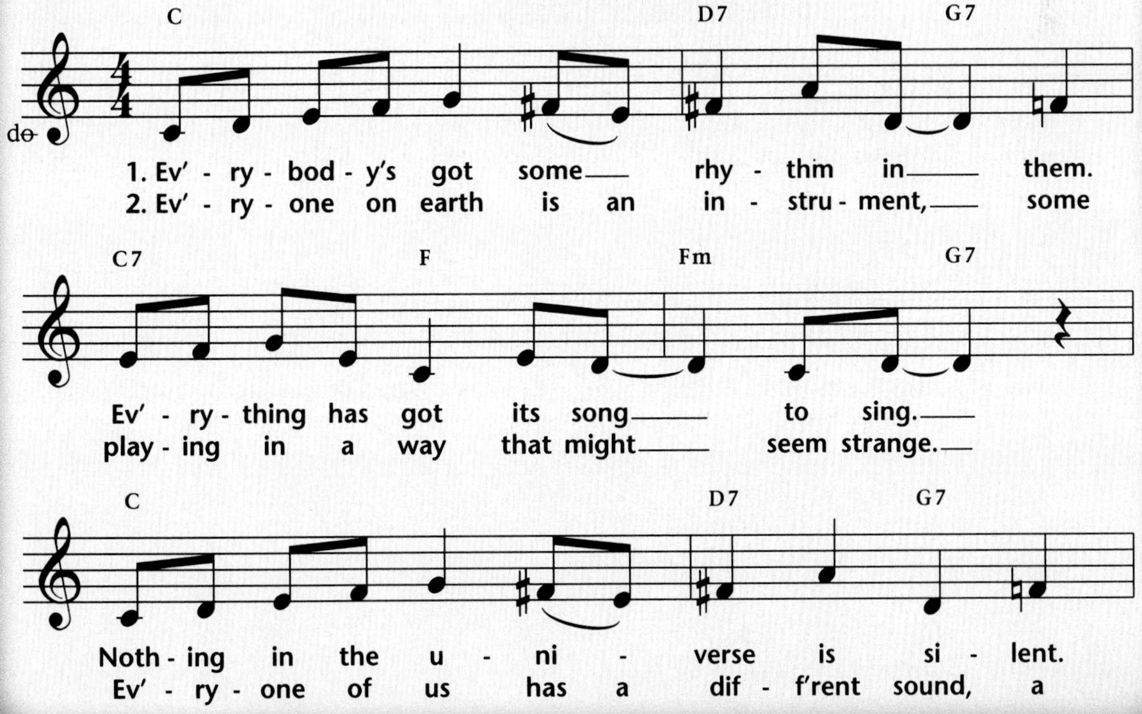

C D7 G7
do
1. Ev' - ry - bod - y's got some rhy - thm in them.
2. Ev' - ry - one on earth is an in - stru - ment, some
C7 F Fm G7
Ev' - ry - thing has got its song to sing.
play - ing in a way that might seem strange.
C D7 G7
Noth - ing in the u - ni - verse is si - lent.
Ev' - ry - one of us has a dif - f'rent sound, a

There's a mel - o - dy in ev' - ry - thing.___
dif - f'rent___ look, a dif - f'rent range.___ If

Ev' - ry - thing ce - les - tial___ is or - ches - tral.
ev' - ry - thing we played were the same old col - or, the

All the stars and plan - ets___ have a voice.
mu - sic that we made sim - ply could-n't be dull - er.

Mu - sic of the spheres can fill our ears and
Deep in you and me is a sym - pho - ny, a

make our hearts___ re - joice!
sym - pho - ny___ of life.

Refrain

Mu - sic! Mu - sic! Lis - ten to the mu - sic!

Any sharp (♯), flat (♭) or natural (♮) that does not appear in the key signature is called an accidental.

NOTICE the accidentals as you sing "Music! Music!" How many accidentals can you find in "Music! Music!"?

JUST FOR THE FUN OF IT

Have you ever sung around a campfire or been part of a group that enjoyed singing together just for entertainment and fun? Songs enjoyed in this way are often **folk songs.** These songs have been passed on from one person to another for such a long time that no one knows who composed them.

There are many styles of folk music. No matter where you go, however, you may hear nonsense songs. "Chumbara" doesn't mean anything, but it's fun to sing!

Brightly

Canadian College Song

The two phrases of "Chumbara" are connected by a scale.
The scale is part of what makes this song fun to sing.

FIND the major scale in the song.

CHORDS CREATE HARMONY

When you hear music, you often hear more than one pitch at a time. This is called harmony. One way to create harmony is with chords. A **chord** is made up of three or more pitches sounding together. People who play instruments such as guitar and keyboards use chords to accompany their melodies.

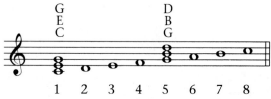

The pitch on which the chord is built is called its **root.** It is often the lowest pitch of the chord. Chords can be named by the letter of the chord root, for example, C chord or G chord. Another way to name chords is by the position of the chord root in the scale.

For example, the chord based on the first step of the scale is also called the I ("one") chord. The chord based on the fifth step of the scale is also called the V ("five") chord. You can accompany many songs, including "Chumbara," with just these two chords.

FIND the chord symbols C and G in "Chumbara." Play the chords on the resonator bells.

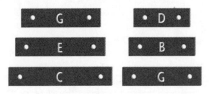

What pitch is in both chords?

SING "Chumbara" as some students play the chords.

FOLK STYLES FROM THE PAST

Go to a Mexican festival and you might sing and dance to "La bamba." This song, which comes from Veracruz, has a catchy rhythm that never fails to get people up on their feet. On this recording you will hear traditional Mexican instruments.

LA BAMBA

Mexican Folk Song

Spanish: **1. Pa - ra bai - lar la bam - ba, pa - ra bai - lar la**
Pronunciation: pa ɾa βai laɾ la bam ba pa ɾa βai laɾ la

(2.) cie - lo, pa - ra su - bir al
sye lo pa ɾa su βiɾ al

bam - ba se ne - ce - si - ta u - na po - ca de gra - cia,
bam ba se ne se si tau na po ka ðe gɾa sia

cie - lo se ne - ce - si - ta u - na es - ca - le - ra gran - de,
sye lo se ne se si tau naes ka le ɾa gɾan de

202

PAT-CLAP to the beat and silently count *1–2.* Pat to the beat as you say *Ba-ma-la-ma Bam!* Then tell which beat has four sounds.

PAT the rhythm of *Ba-ma-la-ma Bam!* during the refrain of "La bamba."

"Oh, my darling, Oh, my darling, Oh, my darling Clementine. . . ." You may have already sung about Clementine, but do you remember when you first heard this song?

The words to "Oh, My Darling, Clementine" mention a "forty-niner," or gold miner from the days of the California Gold Rush, so it might have first been sung around that time. Today it's part of our American folk heritage.

OH, MY DARLING, CLEMENTINE

American Traditional Song

1. In a cav-ern in a can-yon, Ex-ca-vat-ing for a mine,
2. Light she was, so light and air-y, And her shoes were num-ber nine,
3. Drove she duck-lings to the wa-ter, Ev'-ry morn-ing just at nine,
4. Ru-by lips a-bove the wa-ter, Blow-ing bub-bles soft and fine,

Dwelt a min-er, for-ty-nin-er, And his daugh-ter, Clem-en-tine.
Her-ring box-es with-out top-ses, San-dals were for Clem-en-tine.
Hit her foot a-gainst a splin-ter, Fell in-to the foam-ing brine.
But, a-las, I was no swim-mer, So I lost my Clem-en-tine.

Refrain

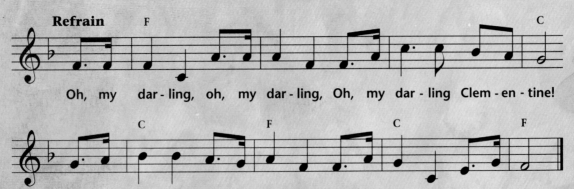

Oh, my dar-ling, oh, my dar-ling, Oh, my dar-ling Clem-en-tine!

You are lost and gone for-ev-er, Dread-ful sor-ry, Clem-en-tine.

"CLEMENTINE" MOVES IN THREES

Find the ¾ meter signature in "Oh, My Darling, Clementine."

The ¾ meter signature in this song means that there are three beats in a measure. The first beat is stressed, followed by two unstressed beats. The quarter note is the symbol for one beat.

Does "Oh, My Darling, Clementine" begin with an upbeat? How many measures are there in each verse up to the refrain?

PRACTICE this ostinato with "Oh, My Darling, Clementine." Snap your fingers on the first two notes. Brush your palms together for the last four notes.

Snap,   snap,   brush brush brush brush.

PLAY the ostinato on instruments. Use two different sounds.

RHYTHM GIVES STYLE

"La bamba" is sung in Spanish. Instruments used to accompany the folk song include the jarocha (Mexican folk harp), a requinto (four-stringed guitar), and a jarana (eight-stringed guitar). These instruments form a conjunto jarocho, a typical ensemble from the port of Veracruz. Percussion effects come from the footwork of the dancers.

PRACTICE the patterns, then play
them together with the song.

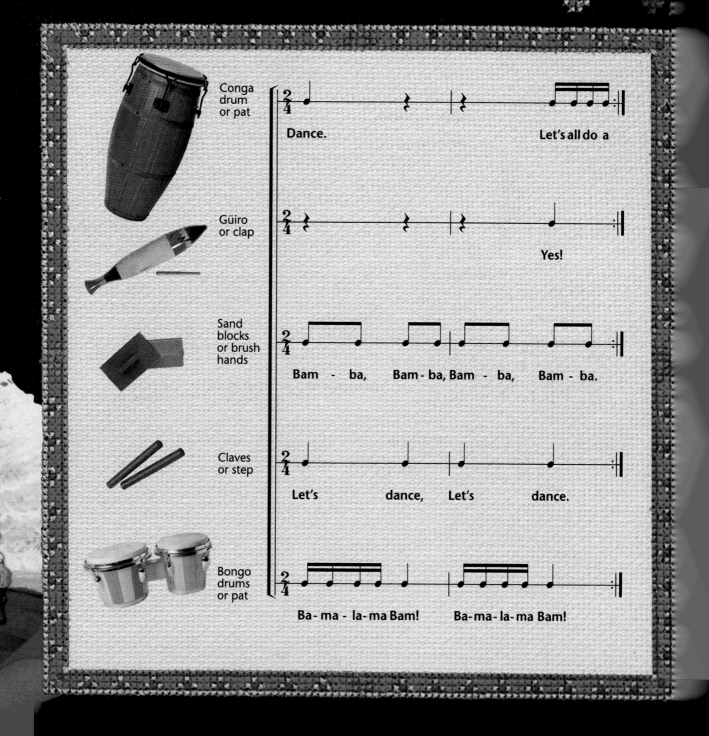

CALYPSO STYLE

"Yellow Bird" sounds like a folk song but it is not. Instead, it is a song composed in a folk style called **calypso.** The composer combined typical Caribbean instruments, syncopated rhythms, and harmonies to give "Yellow Bird" its calypso sound.

Yellow Bird

Music by Norman Luboff
Words by Marilyn Keith and
Alan Bergman

Refrain *mf*
Melody

do

Yel - low bird, up high in___ ba - nan - a tree.

Harmony

do

Yel - low bird, up high in___ ba - nan - a tree.

Yel - low bird, you sit all___ a - lone like me.

Yel - low bird, you sit all___ a - lone like me.

LISTENING

Intrada für Pauken, Trompeten, und Flöten
by Gunild Keetman

An **intrada** *is an opening piece that is festive or marchlike.*

LISTEN for these musical elements in the first section: higher and lower pitches and patterns with four sounds to a beat. Then listen for these differences in tone color and texture in the next sections.

Trumpeten und Pauken

Flöten und Trompete

Flöten, Trompeten, und Pauken

Name the pitched percussion instrument that is used both in "Intrada für Pauken, Trompeten, und Flöten" and "Fanfare for the Common Man."

SPOTLIGHT  *ON*

GUNILD KEETMAN

Gunild Keetman (1904–1990) was a German composer, music educator, and dance teacher. She studied music and dance with Carl Orff, another German composer, and then worked with him to develop materials for teaching music. Her compositions include works for voice, body percussion, Orff instruments, and recorders. Most of her music is found in volumes written especially for students studying music and dance through Orff's philosophy of music education, called Orff-Schulwerk. Throughout her life, Keetman combined teaching music and dance with composing.

Chord Connections

When you learned "Chumbara" you played two chords, C and G—the I and V chords—in the key of C. You can learn to play the I and V chords in other keys and use them to accompany many folk songs.

The I and V chords in the key of F can be played on the resonator bells using the pitches shown.

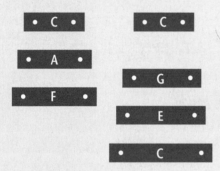

The pitch found in both chords is called the **common tone.** What pitch is the common tone in the F and C chords?

212

A **chord progression** is a series of chords used to harmonize a song. Usually the same chord progression is repeated for each verse.

PRACTICE the following chord progression.

Play the chord progression for each verse of the song "Oh, My Darling, Clementine." Notice that the same chord progression works for the refrain. Once you know the chords and the chord progression, you can accompany this song on any instrument that can produce chords.

SINGING CHORD ROOTS

Did you ever see something you didn't expect? The Biblical prophet Ezekiel saw a vision of wheels within wheels. The spiritual "Ezekiel Saw de Wheel" refers to this event.

LISTEN to "Ezekiel Saw de Wheel" and try to discover where the chord roots are used in the voices. Then listen for the call-and-response style and the sound of the turning wheels.

EZEKIEL SAW DE WHEEL

Allegro Moderato

African American Spiritual

ARRANGING

Rhythms

There are many kinds of careers in music. An **arranger** takes a piece of folk or composed music and makes decisions about how style, instrumentation, tempo, harmony, and dynamics can be changed.

THINK IT THROUGH
How is the work of a composer different from that of an arranger?

Ezekiel Saw de Wheel

LISTENING

Spiritual Arranged by William Dawson

A number of musicians have created their own arrangements of "Ezekiel Saw de Wheel" so that it can be performed in different ways. William Dawson arranged this spiritual for a cappella choir.

COMPARE William Dawson's arrangement of "Ezekiel Saw de Wheel" to the arrangement in your book.

How did William Dawson imitate the sound of wheels turning in his arrangement of "Ezekiel Saw de Wheel"?

TAP the beat and say *doom-a-loom-a* over and over. How many sounds are there to a beat?

Spotlight on William Dawson

William Dawson (1899–1990) was an important American musician. When he was 13, he sold his bicycle for $6.00 to go to Tuskegee Institute in Alabama to learn music. He earned tuition money by working on the school farm. His musical career included being a teacher, conductor, composer, and arranger. Dawson set high standards for himself and insisted on quality performances from his students. He helped others to understand and preserve the African American spiritual.

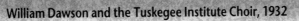

William Dawson and the Tuskegee Institute Choir, 1932

When there are four sounds to a beat, each sound is represented by a sixteenth note (♪). The sixteenth note has two flags. Sixteenth notes in groups of four have a double beam (♬♬). A **sixteenth rest** (𝄿) is the same length as a sixteenth note. How did you imitate the sound of wheels turning when you sang "Ezekiel Saw de Wheel" in two parts?

How would eight sounds to a beat be notated? What would be the name of each of the notes?

NEW RHYTHM COMBINATIONS

Eighth notes and **eighth rests** can be combined with sixteenth notes and sixteenth rests. This makes different rhythm combinations possible. Review these notes and rests.

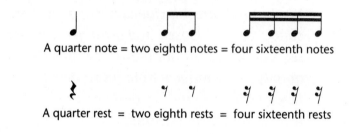

A quarter note = two eighth notes = four sixteenth notes

A quarter rest = two eighth rests = four sixteenth rests

TRY each of these combinations.

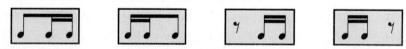

Here is the rhythm notation of a section from "La bamba."

What measures have the ♪♬ pattern?

What measures have the 𝄿♬ pattern?

The painting *American Gothic*, 1930, (far left) is by Grant Wood. Other artists have created new versions of this farm family. Notice the differences and similarities of these pictures.

BE AN ARRANGER

By combining rhythms in your own way, you can experiment with one element of musical style.

CREATE a four-beat pattern with ♩, ♫♫, ♫, and 𝄾 Play your pattern as an accompaniment to "La bamba" or "Ezekiel Saw de Wheel."

THINK IT THROUGH

What other changes could you make to create a new arrangement of "La bamba" or "Ezekiel Saw de Wheel"?

TONE COLORS FROM

The verse of "Chan mali chan" tells about a baby goat who meets people on the road to Kota Bharu. He says, "Love me who has a blue shirt. Love me who has no teeth." It's all in fun! The words *chan mali chan* don't mean anything. People in Asia enjoy this nonsense song just as people in North America enjoy "Chumbara" or "Oh, My Darling, Clementine."

CHAN MALI CHAN

Singaporean Folk Song

Refrain

Malay: Chan ma - li chan, Chan ma - li chan,
Pronunciation: chan ma li chan chan ma li chan

Chan ma - li chan Ke - ti - pung pa - yung.
chan ma li chan kə ti pɔng pa yɔng

Chan ma - li chan, oi! oi! Chan ma - li chan, oi! oi!
chan ma li chan oi oi chan ma li chan oi oi

Chan ma - li chan Ke - ti - pung pa - yung.
chan ma li chan kə ti pɔng pa yɔng

Fine
(3rd time)

THE FAR EAST

Verse

G .... C .... G

1. Di - ma - na di - a   a - nak kam-bing sa - ya
   di   ma   na di   a   a   nak kam bing sa   ya
2. Di - ma - na di - a   a - nak kam-bing sa - ya
   di   ma   na di   a   a   nak kam bing sa   ya

D .... G

A - nak kam-bing sa - ya   per - gi   ke Ko - ta Bha - ru;
a   nak kam bing sa   ya   pə   gi   kə   ko   ta ba   ɾu
A - nak kam-bing sa - ya   ma - kan   te - pi   pe - ri - gi;
a   nak kam bing sa   ya   ma   kan   tə   pi pə   ɾi   gi

G .... C .... G

Di - ma - na di - a   chin - ta ha - ti sa - ya
di   ma   na di   a   chin   ta   ha   ti sa   ya
Di - ma - na di - a   chin - ta ha - ti sa - ya
di   ma   na di   a   chin   ta   ha   ti sa   ya

D .... G   *D.C. al Fine*

chin ta ha - ti sa - ya   yang pa - kai ba - ju bi - ru.
chin ta ha   ti sa   ya   yang pa   kai ba   ju bi   ɾu
chin ta ha - ti sa - ya   yang ti - dak a - da gi - gi.
chin ta ha   ti sa   ya   yang ti   dak a   da gi   gi

The angklung is a pitched percussion instrument used in Singapore. It is made of one or more tuned bamboo tubes set loosely in a frame. The angklung player shakes a tube to produce a specific pitch.

LISTEN for the angklung in "Chan mali chan."

A FOLK SONG FROM KOREA

"Arirang" is one of the most well-known songs from Korea. The song is about the Arirang hill outside of the east gate of Seoul, the capital city of South Korea.

CONDUCT in ¾ as you listen to "Arirang."

1 3   2

ARIRANG

Korean Folk Song
English Words by
Marilyn Davidson

Korean: 아 리 랑 아 리 랑 아 라 리 요
Pronunciation: a ɾi rang a ɾi rang a ɾa ɾi yo
English: A - ri- rang,— A - ri- rang,— A - ra - ri - yo.—

아 리 랑 고 개 를 넘 어 간 다
a ɾi rang go ge ɾul nɔ mɔ gan da
You are go-ing far a-way— o- ver A - ri- rang hill.

나 를 버 리 고 가 시 는 님 은
na ɾul pɔ ɾi go ga shi nɯn ni mɯn
Oh, my friend, if you leave me— here a - lone,— may your

십 리 도 못 가 서 발 병 난 다
shim ni do mo ka sɔ bal pyɔng nan da
feet be- gin to hurt be-fore you've e - ven walked the first mile!

The ornamented version of "Arirang" below includes a changko, which is a Korean drum. The drum has a waist, which means it gets narrow in the center. The body is lacquered wood and the two heads are laced together.

LISTENING

Arirang

Ornamented Version

Korean Folk Song

*Folk songs are passed on from one person to another through singing. In Korea, where "Arirang" is a well-known song, the singer is expected to **ornament**, or decorate, the melody. The ornamentation is different each time, depending on the skill and mood of the singer.*

LISTEN to the ornamented version of "Arirang." The basic melody is the same, but the singer has added extra notes. Then describe how the style of this "Arirang" is different from the one you sang.

AN ACCOMPANIMENT TO "ARIRANG"

CHOOSE three of the rhythm patterns below. Then decide which one to use twice. Place the patterns in any order you like.

Explore drum sounds. Find three different sounds on a drum. Decide how to use these three sounds to perform your four-measure rhythm sequence. Use it to accompany "Arirang."

XYLO-MANIA

AFRICA

Uganda

African musicians use many traditional and modern instruments. Some of the traditional pitched percussion instruments were part of African cultures long before the present-day xylophone was developed.

An amadinda is a traditional log xylophone from Uganda. It is made up of 12 wooden slabs placed horizontally on two logs. Each slab is tuned to a different pitch. The amadinda belongs to the Baganda people who live in the south-central region of Uganda. They play the amadinda on special occasions and during sports and games.

LISTEN to James Makubuya as he speaks about and plays the amadinda and performs "Baamulijja."

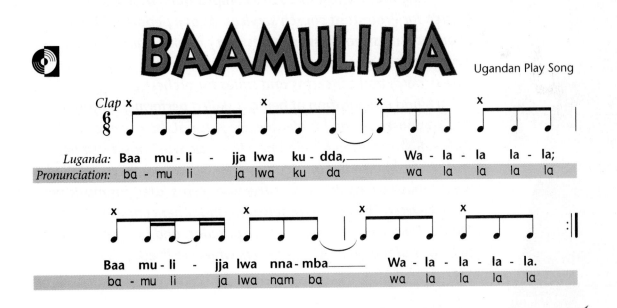

Left to right: bark cloth with stenciled design, grass storage basket, beaded apron from Uganda

LEARN this song from Uganda. The words are in Luganda, the language of the Baganda.

BAAMULIJJA

Ugandan Play Song

Clap **x**

6/8

Luganda: Baa mu-li - jja lwa ku-dda,_____ Wa-la-la la-la;
Pronunciation: ba - mu li ja lwa ku da wa la la la la

Baa mu-li - jja lwa nna-mba_____ Wa-la-la-la-la.
ba - mu li ja lwa nam ba wa la la la la

The words to "Baamulijja" mean: "Be careful; for if you challenge your enemies, make sure you have enough strength to drive them away; otherwise they might destroy you."

Spotlight on

Johann Sebastian Bach

Johann Sebastian Bach (1685–1750) was born over 300 years ago in Germany. Members of Bach's family had been professional musicians for many years. Bach began his musical career at the age of 18, when he took his first job as an organist.

For most of his life, Bach lived quietly and worked very hard at composing music. Most of Bach's compositions were vocal works written for Protestant church services. At one period in his life, he wrote new music for these services every week. In addition, he wrote music for solo instruments such as the violin, flute, and harpsichord, and concertos and suites for orchestras.

Bach had a reputation of being a skilled performer, improviser, and composer during his lifetime. He was not, however, a world-wide celebrity during his lifetime. His music was considered heavy and old-fashioned by some composers. Other composers studied Bach's music for its skilled construction. Years later, his music was "rediscovered" by Felix Mendelssohn and other composers of the 1800s. Today, Bach's music is very popular, and he is considered to be one of the greatest composers who ever lived.

LISTENING

Musette
Harpsichord and Percussion Versions
by Johann Sebastian Bach

Arrangers enjoy giving music a different sound by changing the instruments, rhythms, or harmonies. The music of Johann Sebastian Bach has been arranged in many different ways over the years.

Listen to two versions of "Musette." First, you will hear it on a harpsichord, an instrument used in Bach's time. Then you will hear a new version of the same piece arranged for pitched and unpitched percussion instruments, including the xylophone.

PLAY this "Musette" accompaniment on an unpitched instrument.

The Importance of *Style*

In every culture, people express their feelings through their own music, art, dance, and poetry. The poem "We Return Thanks" is an Iroquois prayer which has been handed down from generation to generation.

WE RETURN THANKS

We return thanks to our Mother, the Earth,
who sustains us—
to the rivers and streams,
that run upon the bosom of the Earth—
to the Three Sisters—corn, beans, and squash—
that support our lives—
to the winds,
that move the air, banishing disease—
to the descending rains,
that give us water and cause all plants to grow—
to the moon and stars,
that give us light when the sun is gone.
We return thanks to the sun,
who looks upon the Earth with a fatherly eye.

—Prayer which opens and closes Iroquois spiritual
  and political gatherings.

THINK IT THROUGH

How can learning poetry and music help you understand people from cultures that are different from your own? What does "We Return Thanks" tell you about the Iroquois culture?

"Tsiothwatasè:tha" is a round dance that came from the tribes of the Plains region to the Iroquois in New York. The Iroquois adapted it to fit their style. The dancers form a circle and alternate movement to the right with movement to the left. Movement to the right stands for good and positive things. Movement to the left symbolizes negative things such as sadness, grief, or anger. According to Iroquois belief, the good always triumphs over the bad and the dance always ends moving to the right.

Tsiothwatasè:tha
ROUND DANCE

Iroquois Social Song and Dance As Sung by Members of the Mohawk Nation

(a)
Mohawk: he yo he yo ha hi yo ha ya
Pronunciation: he yo he yo ha hi yo ha ya

(b)

(c)
he yo ha hi yo ha ya
he yo ha hi yo ha ya

(d)
he yo ha hi yo ha ya
he yo ha hi yo ha ya

(e)
he yo ha hi yo ha ya he yo ha hi yo ha ya
he yo ha hi yo ha ya he yo ha hi yo ha ya

(f)
ho ya he ya ha ho ya he ya ha yo - e (pitch fall off)
ho ya he ya ha ho ya he ya ha yo e

Top left: Turtle Pendant, by Julius Cook, Mohawk Nation (symbolizes story of how the earth, good/evil, and the gifts of the earth came to be). Bottom: Corn Spirit, by Tammy Tarbell, Mohawk Nation. Top right: Water drum and stick, Onondaga Nation.

STYLE BRINGS IT ALL TOGETHER

Styles in music are as different as the earth's peoples. Many factors influence styles, including differences in people, countries, and time periods. In the past, before television, radio, and recordings were invented, people didn't have the opportunity to hear many different styles. Today we can enjoy musical styles from all over the world.

Mickey Hart began drumming at an early age. Both of his parents were drummers. Hart played in rock-and-roll bands, jazz bands, and the Air Force marching band. Since 1967 he has been the percussionist for the rock band The Grateful Dead. Percussion from around the world has become of special interest to him. He has collected percussion instruments as well as the lore and history of drumming in many cultures.

LISTEN to Mickey Hart as he speaks on music of different cultures and the value of all different styles.

"What we call world music really is all the world's music. It's a reflection of our dreams, our lives.... Underneath the world's extraordinary musical diversity is another, deeper realm in which there is no better or worse, no modern or primitive, no art music versus folk music ... but rather a [desire] to translate ... being alive into sound, into rhythm, into something you can dance to."

—*Mickey Hart*, The Planet Drum

Architecture exists in as many styles as music. Notice the variety of forms, colors, and decoration used in these homes. What similarities and differences can you find in the styles of these homes? What other styles of homes have you seen?

REVIEW

SINGING IN STYLE

Imagine that you're on a long hike or car trip with your family or friends. You might enjoy singing a song like "Chumbara" to help pass the time. Listen for the descending major scale as you sing this song.

Another type of folk song is the nonsense ballad. A nonsense ballad tells a story (but not too seriously) and usually there's only a shred of truth in it. "Oh, My Darling, Clementine" is this kind of song. Folk songs are often accompanied by a guitar or banjo strumming chords. Listen for the I and V chords in "Oh, My Darling, Clementine" as you sing it.

Many folk songs are more serious in style. African American spirituals, for example, are songs of faith that originally were often sung a cappella. Today spirituals are sung in a variety of styles. Sing "Ezekiel Saw de Wheel" and think of the qualities that have made spirituals such a valuable part of our American folk heritage.

If you come across Latin American music on the radio, you will probably recognize its distinctive styles. There is a unique character to the way the rhythm, melody, harmony, and tone color are put together and performed. "La bamba" has the added feature of being a dance.

IMPROVISE a dance with a partner using step-touches, turns, and snaps, as you sing "La bamba."

Every one of us has a different sound. This line from "Music! Music!" gives us a clue to the reason that there are so many kinds of music. Sing this song and think about your own musical style. Will it be the same tomorrow as it is today?

CHECK IT OUT

1. Which meter do you hear?

   a. $\frac{3}{4}$ b. $\frac{4}{4}$ c. $\frac{6}{8}$

2. Which meter do you hear?

   a. $\frac{3}{4}$ b. $\frac{4}{4}$ c. $\frac{6}{8}$

3. Which meter do you hear?

   a. $\frac{3}{4}$ b. $\frac{4}{4}$ c. $\frac{6}{8}$

4. Choose the pattern you hear.

5. Choose the pattern you hear.

6. Choose the pattern you hear.

7. Which chord progression do you hear?

   a. I I V I   b. I V I V   c. I V V I   d. I I I V

CREATE

Create an Accompaniment

CREATE accompaniments to "Oh, My Darling, Clementine." Use the chord progression from the song.

Choose a rhythm pattern for the chords. Use one or more of the following patterns or make up your own.

Sing a harmony part. Use the chord roots in the chord progression and add words, for example:

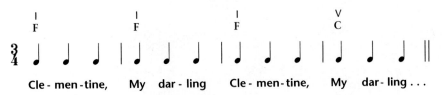

Cle - men - tine,   My   dar - ling   Cle - men - tine,   My   dar - ling . . .

Create and play a countermelody using pitches from the chord progression.

Create a rhythmic ostinato to go with the song. Perform the accompaniments as you sing the song.

Write

Which style of music do you like best? Write a brief paragraph explaining why.

MEXICO LINDO

If you were in Mexico during one of its yearly fiestas, you would enjoy the ringing of bells, exciting fireworks, and tasty refreshments. You might also enjoy the popular folk dances.

Some of the dancers might be performing the *jarabe*. This Mexican dance was influenced by Spanish colonists who brought their native dances and songs to Mexico. It is still part of the Mexican tradition for young people to learn the dance.

Mexican dancers at a festival in San Antonio, Texas

LISTENING

El jarabe tapatío

Listen to a jarabe from Jalisco, a state in Western Mexico. The music of the jarabe is in several parts. Each part has a different rhythm and melody and different movements.

IDENTIFY changes in the melody and the rhythm.

Las Chiapanecas

LISTENING

The lively and rapid sounds of "Las Chiapanecas" (The Women from Chiapas) invite the audience to clap the rhythm of the music. "Las Chiapanecas" also features the zapateado. This is a solo dance done in triple time that requires the dancer to use strong foot and heel movements.

LISTEN and clap to the rhythm of "Las Chiapanecas."

Meet Linda Ronstadt

Born in Tucson, Arizona, Linda Ronstadt grew up in a musical family. Her father played the guitar and sang Mexican songs. Her mother played the ukulele, and the whole family enjoyed listening to music and singing. Ronstadt, who calls herself a "pop singer with rock and roll roots," began her career as a professional singer in 1967. She received Grammy Awards in 1993 for the Best Tropical Latin and Mexican/American Albums.

LISTEN to Linda Ronstadt talk about her career.

A *corrido* is a Mexican epic poem or folk ballad. The subject of the songs in a corrido can be any interesting event, past or present. Thousands of these songs have been written, and more are being written all the time. The songs are usually in rhymed verse and performed to guitar accompaniment.

SING a corrido, "El quelite."

In this song, there are two meanings for *quelite*. It is a village (*el quelite*) and a wild green plant (*verde quelite*).

El quelite

The Village

Mexican Folk Song
English Words by MMH

Spanish:	Al	pie	de un	ver- de	que-	li- te	me	dio	sue- ño	y	me	dor-
Pronunciation:	al	pye	ðe un	ßeɾ de	ke	li te	me	ðyo	swe	nyoi	me	ðoɾ
English:	At the	edge	of	a green__	*que-*	*li- te,*	I	stopped	a- while	there	to	

	mí,	y me	des- per- tó	un	ga- lli- to		can- tan- do	"qui qui ri
	mi	ime	ðes peɾ to	un	ga yi to		kan tan do	ki ki ɾi
	sleep.	A	roos- ter	cried out	and woke me.	He	sang a	"qui qui ri

quí." Yo no can-to por-que si pue-do, ni por que mi voz se-a
ki yono kan to poɾ ke si pweðo nipoɾ ke miβos se a
quí." I don't sing be-cause I'm a-ble, nor be-cause my voice is

bue-na, can-to por-que ten-go gus-to en mi tie-rra y en la a-
βwe na kan to poɾ ke teng go gus to enmi tye ɾa i en laa
good. I sing be-cause I feel joy in my land and for-eign

je-na. Ma-ña-na, me voy ma-ña-na, ma-ña-na me voy de a-
xe na ma nya na me βoi ma nya na ma nya na me βoi ðea
lands. To-mor-row I will be leav-ing, and who can tell where I'll

quí, y el con-sue-lo que me que-da que se han de a-cor-dar de mi.
ki ɰel kon swe lo ke me ke ða ke sean ðea koɾ ðaɾ ðe mi
be? But here is my con-so-la-tion: that some-one re-mem-bers me.

WRITE your own verse about life in a small village.

PRESENT your verse for "El quelite" to the class.

The Yesterdays and the Tomorrows

No year stands by itself,
any more than any day stands alone.
There is the continuity of all the years
in the trees,
the grass,
even in the stones on the hilltops.
Even in man.
For time flows like water,
eroding and building,
shaping and ever flowing;
and time is a part of us,
not only our years, as we speak of them,
but our lives,
our thoughts.
All our yesterdays are summarized in our now,
and all the tomorrows are ours
to shape.

—Hal Borland

LOOKING BACK

LOOKING FORWARD

FORMING THE FUTURE

Looking back on music from earlier times can help you better understand music of both today and yesterday. Listen for ways that music of long ago is like music that was written recently. Think about how music may change in the future. One of the elements of music that you find in every time period is **form**, the way a composer organizes musical material.

LOOK for form in "Young People of the World." Locate the two main sections and the canon at the end.

Young People of the World

Words and
Music by
Glen Everhart

Em

D

1. Young peo - ple of the world, put your hands to - geth-
2. Young peo - ple of the world, put your minds to - geth-

Em   D   Em

- er, put your hands to - geth - er, young peo - ple.
- er, put your minds to - geth - er, young peo - ple.

Em   D

Young peo - ple of the world, put your hearts to - geth-
Young peo - ple of the world, put your dreams to - geth-

- er, put your hearts to - geth - er, young peo - ple.
- er, put your dreams to - geth -

- er, young peo - ple. Got - ta shout! up to the sky, ——

you got - ta show ev' - ry - bod - y there's a rea - son —— why, ——

you got - ta raise your voi - ces —— all o - ver the world ——

D.C. (2nd time to Canon)

and let your spir - it —— shine! ——

Canon

Young peo - ple of the world, put your { hands hearts minds dreams } to - geth -

- er, put your { hands hearts minds dreams } to - geth - er, young peo - ple. Shout!

LISTENING

String Quartet

Op. 33, No. 3, Fourth Movement

by Franz Joseph Haydn

The string quartet is made up of two violins, a viola, and a cello. Composers started writing for this combination in the 1700s. Franz Joseph Haydn developed the string quartet into its distinctive form and wrote over 80 string quartets.

*Composers use repetition and contrast to make their music interesting. **Rondo** is a musical form based on these ideas of same and different. The sections of a rondo may be organized as:*
A B A C A or A B A C A B A or A B A C A D A.

The Granger Collection

Lithograph from the 1800s, showing an 18th century Austrian string quartet

LISTEN for repetitions of the A section and the contrasting B and C sections in the fast-moving Fourth Movement from String Quartet Op. 33, No. 3.

This song is an interesting mix of past and present. It is sung both in Samoan, a traditional Polynesian language, and in English, a language that is relatively new to the islands. "Savalivali" is used today in Samoan schools where students are learning English.

LISTEN closely to how "Savalivali" is performed. What musical form is used in this song?

Savalivali

Samoan Folk Song
Collected and
Transcribed by
Kathy B. Sorensen

NOTICE the dotted eighth and sixteenth rhythm (♪♫). A *dotted eighth note* lasts as long as three sixteenth notes tied together. What other song in this lesson uses ♪♫ ?

BLUES,
HOW DO YOU DO?

Did you ever use the expression "I'm feeling blue"? It means that you're not happy. A style of music called the **blues** grew out of the sorrow and troubled feelings of Africans who were enslaved and brought to this country. Music in the blues style started in the early 1900s and is still popular today.

LISTENING

Good Mornin', Blues *by Huddie Ledbetter*

Like many other blues singers, Huddie Ledbetter often played the guitar to accompany his singing.

LISTEN to Ledbetter sing "Good Mornin', Blues."

Spotlight on LEADBELLY

"Singin' the blues" came naturally to Huddie Ledbetter (1885–1949), better known as "Leadbelly." Leadbelly had a hard life. By the age of 15 he had learned to play a twelve-stringed guitar and was supporting himself by singing on the streets of Dallas, Texas. He memorized hundreds of work and game songs, field hollers, ballads, and other songs. Leadbelly was first "discovered" in the early 1930s and from then until the time of his death, he performed these same traditional songs.

246

GOOD MORNIN' BLUES

Words and Music by
Huddie Ledbetter

1. Good morn - in', blues;____
2. I lay down last night,____

Blues, how do you do?____
turn - in' from side to side.____

Good morn - in', blues;____ Blues, how do you do?____
Yes, I was turn - in' from side to side.____

I'm do - ing all right,____ good morn - in', how are you?
I was not____ a - sleep,____ but I was dis - sat - is - fied.

Good Mornin', Blues. New words and new music arrangement by Huddie Ledbetter. Edited with new additional material by
Alan Lomax. TRO © Copyright 1959 (renewed) Folkways Music Publishers, Inc., New York, NY. Used by permission.

A SOUND AND A STYLE

The blues style is more than just singing about sad times. The blues have a distinctive musical flavor that is created by singing or playing pitches that have been "bent." These are called **blue notes.** Most people who sing the blues never give a thought to these blue notes; they just sing them automatically. Those who want to write down these notes show the altered pitches with accidentals.

The flatted blue notes create the sound of the blues scale. This scale is somewhat like a major scale with two or three added notes. The lowered third, seventh, and sometimes fifth degrees of the scale are the most commonly used blue notes.

Major scale
1 2 3 4 5 6 7 8

Blues scale
1 2 3 4 5 6 7 8

IDENTIFY the blue note in the melody of "Good Mornin', Blues."

The blues continues to influence jazz and much popular music. Here, for example, is "Jazz Round." What blue notes and other accidentals do you find in this song?

JAZZ ROUND

Words and Music by
John Coates

Notice the unusual words for this song. These nonsense words, called **scat syllables,** are popular with jazz singers. They allow the singers to use their voices like instruments.

THINK IT THROUGH
"Jazz Round" has a flatted third and seventh step of the scale. Does that mean that it is in the blues style?

Manhattan Transfer uses scat syllables in some of their songs.

TEMPO TRAVELS

Chamber music is music usually played by a small ensemble. Chamber ensembles come in different sizes and are made up of different instruments. Here is a **woodwind quintet**. How is it different from a string quartet? Is there any similarity between the two chamber ensembles?

flute

oboe

French horn

bassoon

THINK IT THROUGH
Why do you think the French horn is part of a "woodwind" ensemble?

LISTENING

Suite for Wind Quintet
First Movement
by Ruth Crawford-Seeger

*The first movement of "Suite for Wind Quintet" has three sections:
A B A. This pattern occurs in each section.*

$\frac{10}{8}(\frac{6}{8}+\frac{2}{4})$ ♪. ♪ ₇ ♪ ♪ ♪ ₇ ♪ ♫ ♪ ♫ ‖

Listen for these changes.

A   Pattern acts as an ostinato in the bassoon

B   Instruments play modified pattern in octaves

*A   Transformation of the pattern in the oboe,
then flute, and finally the bassoon*

*There is something more than just a change in instruments that
marks off these three sections. What is it?*

clarinet

SPOTLIGHT ON
Ruth Crawford-Seeger

*Ruth Crawford-Seeger (1901–
1953) wrote "Suite for
Wind Quintet" in 1952.
At the time she wrote it
she was best known
for her collections of
American folk songs
for children. From
1926, when she was
25 years old, until
her death in 1953, she
was a teacher and an
active composer of music
for small orchestra, piano,
chamber ensembles, and voice. Her
music was ahead of its time because of her bold
technique and was rarely performed during her
lifetime. Only since her death have her compositions been widely recognized.*

Tempo is an Italian word that means "the speed of the beat." Tempo markings are used to describe the tempo the composer wants for a particular piece of music. These words are often found above the first line of music and anywhere the tempo changes. Tempo markings are most often found in Italian. Other languages such as German, English, and French, are also used. Look for tempo markings in music you perform.

belebt
(brisk)

moderato
(moderate)

largo
(broad)

accelerando
(quickening)

ritardando
(slowing)

adagio
(at ease)

allegro
(fast)

andante
(walking)

plodding

allegretto
(lively)

THINK IT THROUGH

What other words besides the ones on this page could be used as tempo markings?

REVIEW "Tsiothwatasè:tha" and describe the tempo.

lento
(slow)

presto
(very fast)

prestissimo
(as fast as possible)

go like crazy

Meet
ARLIENE
NOFCHISSEY
WILLIAMS

Arliene Nofchissey Williams is a Navaho from Arizona. In 1967, she and Carnes Burson, a Ute, composed the song "Go, My Son" while they were attending Brigham Young University. They wrote it for a Native American student touring group.

Williams explains that "Go, My Son" was written to encourage Native American youth to continue their education past high school. She says that education for Native Americans is also in nature, where they can learn from the trees, the mountains, the sun, the rain, the wind, and all the elements.

LISTEN as Arliene Nofchissey Williams tells about the meaning of "Go, My Son."

FIND the tempo markings in the notation of "Go, My Son" and use both of them when you perform the song. *Andante* means "at a moderate walking tempo," and *ritardando* (*rit.*) means "to slow down."

This silver-and-turquoise necklace was made in 1992 by Alice Blackgoat, a Navaho. The skills to make this squash-blossom necklace have been passed from generation to generation.

GO, MY SON

Words and Music by
Carnes Burson and
Arliene Nofchissey Williams

Andante

1. Go, my son, go and climb the lad-der. Go, my son,
2. Work, my son, get an ed-u-ca-tion. Work, my son,
(3.) on the lad-der of an ed-u-ca-tion, You can see to

go and earn your fea-ther. Go, my son,
learn a good vo-ca-tion and Climb, my son,
help your In-dian na-tion then Reach, my son, and

Gb

1. Db

make your peo-ple proud of you._____
go and take a loft-y
lift your peo-ple up with

2. Db

view._____ 3. From you.

3. Db D

Go, my son,
on the lad-der

D   Bm   *Second time to Coda* ⊕

go and climb the lad-der. Go, my son,   go and earn your fea - ther.
of an ed-u-ca-tion, You can see to help your In-dian na-tion, then

Em   G   D

Go, my son, make your peo-ple proud of you._____ From

Coda
⊕ Em   *rit.*   G   D

Reach, my son and lift your peo-ple up with you.

Musette *(performed by Yo-Yo Ma and Bobby McFerrin)*
by Johann Sebastian Bach

LISTENING

"Musette" is performed by a cellist and singer. Think back and remember this music, but look forward to a new sound!

SHOW the tempo as you listen to "Musette."

What happened to the tempo? How did Bobby's voice change in the song?

FORM A NEW CHORD

When it comes to accompanying the blues, the guitar player usually plays more chords than melody. The blues harmony is usually built around the I, IV, and V chords. These are the chords built on the first, fourth, and fifth steps of the scale. "Good Mornin', Blues" is in F major, so the I, IV, and V chords are F, Bb, and C. The root of each chord is given below.

IDENTIFY the names of the other pitches in each chord.

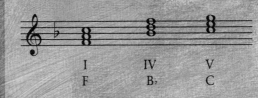

Harmony in the blues is usually provided by a specific chord progression called a blues progression. One of the most characteristic blues progressions is twelve measures, or bars, long. That's why it is called the **twelve-bar blues.** On the right is the chord sequence for "Good Mornin', Blues."

256

SING the chord roots as you listen to the twelve-bar blues progression of "Good Mornin', Blues."

Good Mornin', Blues

Words and Music
by Huddie Ledbetter

4/4	1 I I I I F Good | morn - in', blues; _____	2 I I I I F Blues, how do you do? _____	3 I I I I F _____	4 I I I I F Good
	5 IV IV IV IV B♭ morn - in', blues; _____	6 IV IV IV IV B♭ Blues, how do you do?	7 I I I I F _____	8 I I I I F I'm
	9 V V V V C do-ing all right, __good	10 IV IV IV IV B♭ morn - in', how are	11 I I I I F you? _____	12 I I I F

Rondeau
from *Symphonies de Fanfares*, No. 1
by Jean-Joseph Mouret

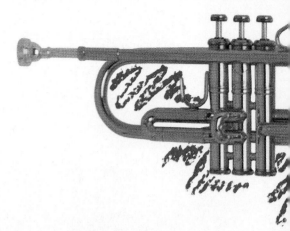

In the 1700s, a French composer, Jean-Joseph Mouret, wrote a rondeau, or rondo. It is played by a **brass quintet** *like the one below. How is this chamber ensemble different from the woodwind quintet? Which musical instrument is used in both quintets?*

trumpet   French horn   tuba   trombone   trumpet

COUNT the number of times the A section occurs as you listen to "Rondeau." What instrument plays the theme? Is "Rondeau" a rondo?

A RONDO?

Listen again to "Savalivali." Is it in rondo form? Explain why or why not. List the sections.

MOVE to "Savalivali," choosing a different movement for each section.

Look at this picture. How do you suppose he feels? What might have happened? Have you ever looked this way? Could he be having a case of "the blues"?

CREATE **your own blues lyrics, or words.**

The first thing you need is the feeling—something you can "feel blue" about. How do you choose a topic? What about the time you had three tests on the same day? What about when your best friend moved to another city? Or when your dog died?

Now that you have the idea, you need to know about the rhyme scheme of blues lyrics. Look at the lyrics of "Joe Turner Blues."

JOE TURNER Blues

American Blues

1. They tell me—— Joe Turn-er's—— come and gone.——
2. He came here—— with for-ty—— links of chain.——

They tell me—— Joe Turn-er's—— come and gone.——
He came here—— with for-ty—— links of chain.——

He left me—— here to sing—— this—— song.
He left me—— here to sing—— this—— song.

Notice the rhyme scheme of "Joe Turner Blues." Two identical lines are followed by a different line that rhymes. Each line fits into the same number of beats.

Does "Joe Turner Blues" have the same form as "Good Mornin', Blues"?

Use this rhyme scheme as a model to write your own blues lyrics. Then sing the lyrics to the melody of "Good Mornin', Blues." Remember, your new lyrics will need to have about the same number of syllables as "Good Mornin', Blues" to fit the melody.

When you have written your blues lyrics, you're ready to "sing the blues."

ACCOMPANY yourself or a friend with the twelve-bar blues chord progression. Use the F, B♭, and C chords as the I, IV, and V chords.

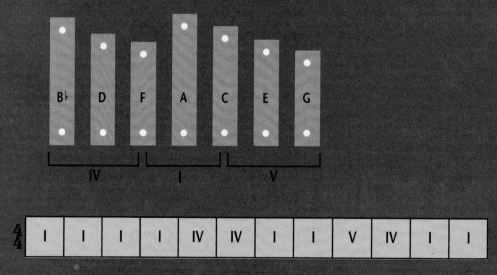

CHOOSE instruments for your blues piece. Use instruments and players that are available. You may want to include a part for someone who plays an instrument such as flute, trumpet, or clarinet.

PAST AND @ PRESENT RHYTHMS

Flamenco dancer from Spain

"Canten, señores cantores" is a song from the northern part of Argentina. Notice the rhythms in the song. The sixteenth-eighth-sixteenth (♪♩♪) rhythm is twice as fast as the ♪♩ ♪ syncopated pattern.

Argentine guitarist

PRACTICE these rhythm patterns. They appear in songs both old and new.

1. $\frac{2}{4}$

2. $\frac{2}{4}$

3. $\frac{2}{4}$

4. $\frac{2}{4}$

Canten, señores cantores

Sing, Gentlemen Singers

Argentine Traditional Song
English Words by MMH

Spanish: Can - ten se - ño - res can - to - res lo que ve - ní - an can - tan - do;
Pronunciation: kan ten se nyo res kan to res lo ke βe ni an kan tan do
English: Sing, now, *se - ño - res can - to - res,* you, who have come to sing your song.

Yo co - mo re - cién lle - ga - do al - zo mi voz con re - ce - lo.
yo ko mo re syen ye ga ðo al so mi βos kon re se lo
Though I am hes - i - tant and shy, I raise my voice and sing a - long.

Na - ran - ja - les, du - raz - na - les, que bo - ni - tos car - na - va - les.
na ran xa les ðu ras na les ke βo ni tos kar na βa les
Or - an - ges sweet, peach - es to eat; beau - ti - ful is car - ni - val time!

What are some contemporary Hispanic groups today? What songs have they made popular in your area?

Gloria Estefan and Miami Sound Machine

WRITTEN RHYTHMS, OLD AND NEW

If you compare the score for a song written in the time of Haydn with one written in your lifetime, you'll see that they both communicate the rhythm by note values and rests.

Haydn String Quartet

"Young People of the World"

TWO HORSES

Compare the two sculptures. One was created over 2500 years ago. The other was made recently. How are the sculptures the same? How are they different?

Horse, sixth century B.C., Terra-cotta, 5 1/4" tall Greek

Ferdinand, 1990
Found Steel, 77″ tall
Deborah Butterfield

Music from very different times and places can have the same rhythm patterns.

LOOK at the notation fragments below. Can you tell, just by looking, which comes from an Argentine song or which comes from a Mohawk song? Can you tell which one is Samoan?

CLAP each rhythm and see if you can identify the song.

THE PAST AND blues

One of the musical elements that gives the blues its special sound is the bass line. The bass line is often played in such a way that it seems to sing out almost as much as the melody. Often the root of each chord is used as a bass note. What are the roots of the I, IV, and V chords below?

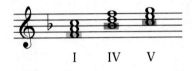

I   IV   V

LISTEN to "Good Mornin', Blues," and point to the root of the appropriate chord as it is played. How many times did you hear the B♭ used as the root? What about the C?

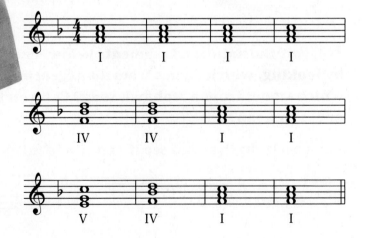

A bass line is often played by a string bass (left) or an electric bass (right).

PRESENT

Musicians have all kinds of tricks to make a bass line come alive. Sometimes the bass line is heard all by itself as a solo, then other instruments join in to make the harmony complete.

Below is a bass line pattern to play with "Good Mornin', Blues" or your own blues. It is based on the same chord progression you learned earlier.

PLAY these *arpeggios*, which are "**broken**" chords.

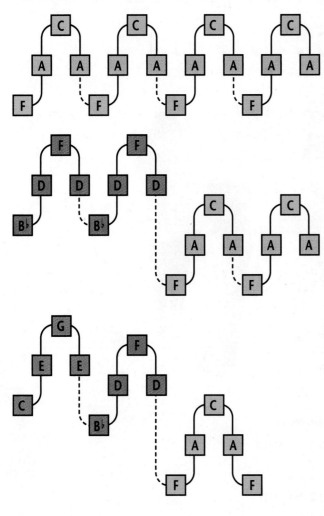

You have learned about rondo form and blues harmony. Now combine these two elements to create a new blues rondo.

LEARN this rap as the A section.

A RHYME IN TIME

Words and Music by René Boyer-White

With a Swing

Let's clap ev'-ry-bod-y, it is time to show

That you can say a rhyme in time and keep the flow.

It won't be ea-sy, I can guar-an-tee.

Shake the blues! All to-geth-er now, 1 2 3.

USE the original blues lyrics you created for your B section.

USE an original jazzy body-percussion pattern for your C section, or use a short poem or rhyme.

ACCOMPANY the B section of the rondo with the twelve-bar blues bass line.

Meet BRUCE UCHITEL

You might hear someone call out to a group of jazz instrumentalists, "Speak to me" or "Sing it." That means that the players seem to talk and sing through their instruments.

Bruce Uchitel (b. 1951) is a free-lance guitarist and arranger. He has played in Broadway musicals such as Cats and Les Miserables. Uchitel has arranged and played on some recordings for this book. When he plays the blues, he can "bend" pitches by pushing or pulling on the guitar strings to make the instrument "speak."

LISTEN to Bruce Uchitel as he speaks and plays, and decide whether or not he makes his instrument "speak the blues."

Parker's Mood by Charlie Parker

LISTENING

Through music, performers can communicate the feelings of others. Barry Harris, a jazz pianist, does this in his "laid back" rendition of "Parker's Mood," a piece written by the great jazz saxophonist, Charlie Parker.

LISTEN to "Parker's Mood" and try to follow the blues progression. See if you agree that it still has a feeling of the blues, even though the blues progression is used in a different way.

The LOUD and SOFT of It

You've heard of people described as being "dynamic," but what does that mean? What is a dynamic person? That person is on the move, energetic, changing.

That description also applies to dynamics in music. The changes in intensity and loudness of the sound are called **dynamics.**

The words and symbols that tell you how loud or how soft to play the music are called dynamic marks. Most of the words are in Italian.

FIND the dynamic marks below.

fortissimo (very loud)
forte (loud)
mezzo forte (medium loud)
mezzo piano (medium soft)
piano (soft)
pianissimo (very soft)

pp p mp mf f ff   *ff f mf mp p pp*

crescendo
(getting louder)

decrescendo
(getting softer)

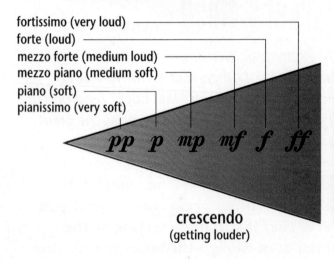

YOUTH

Even though you may not be aware of it, you use dynamics in your everyday conversation. When you call out a greeting or whisper a secret, you are using extremes of dynamics.

READ the lines from the poem, using dynamic variations. Try some contrasts in dynamics and ask a partner what the effect was.

We have tomorrow
Bright before us
Like a flame.

Yesterday
A night-gone thing,
A sun-down name.

And dawn-today
Broad arch above the road we came.

We march!

—Langston Hughes

Sail into your future with this song.

SING "Sail Away" using different dynamics to make the music expressive.

 # SAIL AWAY

Finnish Folk Song
New Words Arranged by
Elizabeth Gilpatrick

Verses 1, 3: unison   Verses 2, 4: canon

1. Who can sail a - way with no wind?
2. Who can fly to the top of the hill?
3. I can sail a - way with no wind,
4. I can fly to the top of the hill,

Who can row with - out oars?
Who can reach the sky?
I can reach the sky,
I can reach the sky,

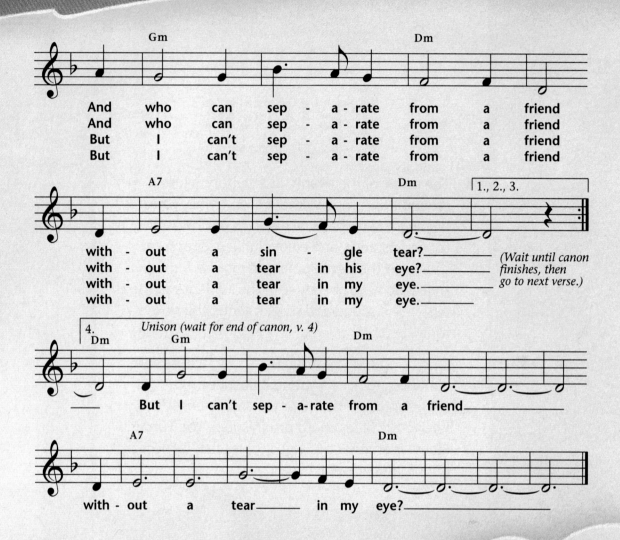

THINK IT THROUGH

Describe the dynamics, tempo, and style in "Sail Away." Then compare the dynamics, tempo, and style of "Sail Away" with "Good Mornin', Blues" or "Joe Turner Blues."

Take your past with you and with it build your future. Sail away and take music with you!

To the Future!

The music of the twenty-first century is just around the corner. Without even trying, you are helping it take shape. What each person listens to, understands, and enjoys influences in some small way the development of musical form and style. You have already seen the influence of the past in the sound and style of songs you sing today.

Sing "Good Mornin', Blues," a song whose style continues to have a strong influence on the music of today. Listen for the characteristic twelve-bar blues chord progression. "Joe Turner Blues" is another twelve-bar blues that came out of the same era.

"Jazz Round" uses blue notes, but it is not in the twelve-bar blues form or blues style. Blue notes have been used in the early blues as well as more modern jazz styles. Listen for the blue notes as you sing "Jazz Round" in canon.

Rondo form has been popular for centuries. Listen for the return of the A section in the fourth movement of String Quartet Op. 33, No. 3 by Franz Joseph Haydn.

A blending of the old and new happens in music from all over the world. In the Samoan song "Savalivali," the traditional Samoan language is combined with English, a language newer to these islands.

Looking back, looking forward. Take all you can from the past and the present with you into the future. Let it give you insight, understanding, and vision. Sing "Young People of the World." In what way do you most want to change the world of the future?

CHECK IT OUT

1. Choose the form that you hear.

   a. A B A   **b.** A B A C A   **c.** A B   **d.** A A B A

2. Choose the form that you hear.

   a. A B A C A   **b.** A B   **c.** A B A   **d.** A B C

3. Choose the form that you hear.

   a. A B   **b.** A B A   **c.** A A B A   **d.** A B A C A

4. Which chord progression do you hear?

   a. I IV V I   **b.** I V IV I   **c.** I IV I V   **d.** I I IV V

5. Which chord progression do you hear?

   a. I V IV V   **b.** I IV IV I   **c.** I IV V I   **d.** I V IV I

CREATE

Create and Perform a Rondo

Work in a small group to create a rondo. Choose a short song or part of a longer song for the A section. Use its subject as a theme for your rondo. Let your choices for the other sections be guided by what is appropriate to express your theme.

CREATE music for the B and C sections. You may design a percussion piece with rhythm only, make up a melody to fit the blues chord progression, or use a poem that expresses your theme. The sections should be roughly the same length.

Choose instruments and voices to perform each part. Practice each section with your group.

ORGANIZE the sections into rondo form. Choose one of the following: A B A C A B A, A B A C A, A B A C A D A.

Write

What will the music of the future be like? Imagine that you are a music critic attending a concert sometime after the year 2010. Write a review of the performance, including as many details as possible about the music and musicians.

Encore NEW VOICES:

Musicians in our time often know as much about computers as they do about music. Computers, digital recording, and electronic instruments are changing the way many musicians create sounds.

Pitches, rhythms, dynamics, tempo, and other musical information can now be processed through a computer device called MIDI, or **M**usic **I**nstrument **D**igital **I**nterface. A composer can play music on a keyboard or other MIDI-connected instrument into a computer. The computer remembers what was played and can play it back exactly as it "learned" it. The composer can then play second, third, or more additional parts, and the computer can remember them all. It can then play the music back, becoming an electronic orchestra.

LISTENING

Brandenburg Concerto No. 3 Allegro

by J. S. Bach, arranged by James Roberts

Bach wrote his Brandenburg Concerto No. 3 in 1721 for an orchestra of string instruments. Each of the string sections has a different part to play, and the lines of the various parts interweave to make a tapestry of orchestral sound.

More than 250 years later, James Roberts, an American composer and electronic musician, took the parts of Bach's piece and played them into a computer one at a time. Like Bach, Roberts assigned a different instrument to each part, but these are electronic instruments that will perform through the memory of the computer. In effect, Roberts became a one-man electronic orchestra, creating a new and modern tapestry from a traditional piece of music.

Making Music with Technology

▲ Computer technology has made it possible for composers to hear the sound of their instrumental music and revise it on the spot.

LISTEN to Roberts' computer-generated arrangement of Bach's concerto.

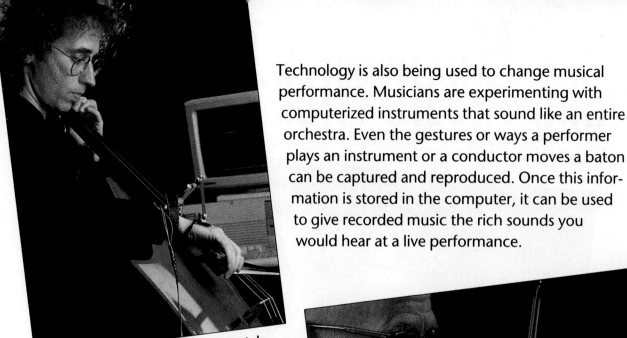

Technology is also being used to change musical performance. Musicians are experimenting with computerized instruments that sound like an entire orchestra. Even the gestures or ways a performer plays an instrument or a conductor moves a baton can be captured and reproduced. Once this information is stored in the computer, it can be used to give recorded music the rich sounds you would hear at a live performance.

▲ Tod Machover, of the M.I.T. Media Lab, enters hand movement information for playing the cello into the computer.

▶ Max Matthews, of Stanford University, plays an electronic violin.

LISTENING Cannon River Wave/Forms (excerpt) *by David Means*

The development of computer technology has enabled composers to put together sound sources in new and creative ways. Often, composers combine computer-generated sounds with live performances. In an outdoor performance in Northfield, Minnesota, musicians and sound engineers worked together to create a public art event. The natural sounds of the Cannon River were used as a backdrop for a sound event that included computers, electronic and acoustic instruments, live environmental sounds, and voices. In the score, the composer used the symbols on page 283.

Composers and conductors of the future will be able to choose from a large selection of musical and vocal styles, instruments, and orchestra size. But if they are not able to find what they are looking for, there will be special computers that will take orders and supply the desired sounds.

▲ Max Matthews uses radio wands to conduct an orchestra.

▶ The complex movements of a conductor's hands are made visible so that they can be analyzed and studied.

CREATE your own sound event using the recording of "Cannon River Wave/Forms."

Listen to the music. Use the symbols in the chart to make a map of the sounds you hear.

⌒	High sweeps	◇	Whistle tones
✳	"Twinkle" tones	⁝	Low pulses and explosions
⬛	Singing and spoken voices		

Decide what sounds you will add, using classroom instruments or vocal sounds. Note these in your map, using symbols of your own. Perform from your map using the recording as background.

CELEBRATION

I shall dance tonight.
When the dusk comes crawling,
There will be dancing
    and feasting.
I shall dance with the others
      in circles,
        in leaps,
          in stomps.
Laughter and talk will
    weave into the night,
Among the fires
    of my people.
Games will be played
And I shall be
    a part of it.

               —*Alonzo Lopez*

Hooray for the RED, WHITE, AND BLUE

The 50 states that make up the United States are each special in their own way—from Alaska, the northernmost state, to Hawaii, the southernmost. However, one thing that many of the states have in common is a name with Native American origins. The name Alaska, for example, came from *alakshak,* an Inuit word for "peninsula," "great lands," or "land that is not an island."

★ ★ ★ FIFTY NIFTY ★ ★ ★
UNITED STATES

Words and Music
by Ray Charles

Fif-ty nif-ty U-nit-ed States from thir-teen o-rig-i-nal col-o-nies;

Fif-ty nif-ty stars in the flag that bil-lows so beau-ti-f'ly in— the breeze.

Each in - di - vid - u - al state con - tri - butes a qual - i - ty that is great.

Each in - di - vid - u - al state de - serves a bow, we sa - lute them now.

Fif - ty nif - ty U - ni - ted States from thir - teen o - rig - i - nal col - o - nies,

Shout 'em, scout 'em, Tell all a - bout 'em, One by one till we've

giv - en a day to ev' - ry state in the U. S. A. Al - a -

2nd time as fast as possible

bam - a A - las - ka, Ar - i - zo - na, Ar - kan - sas, Cal - i -

for - nia, Col - o - ra - do, Con - nect - i - cut; Del - a - ware,

288 HOORAY FOR THE RED, WHITE, AND BLUE

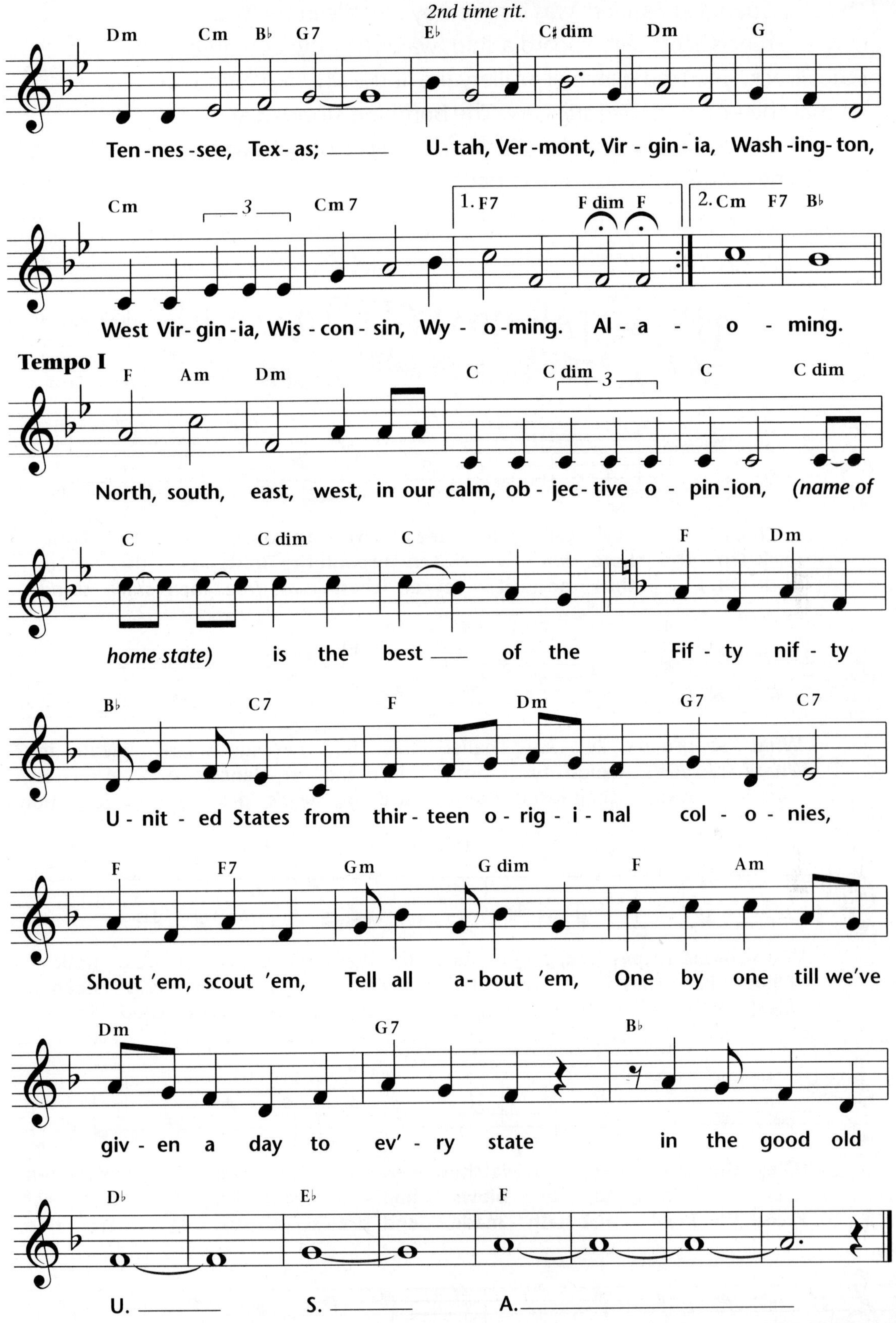
2nd time rit.
Dm Cm B♭ G7 E♭ C♯dim Dm G
Ten-nes-see, Tex-as; U-tah, Ver-mont, Vir-gin-ia, Wash-ing-ton,
Cm 3 Cm7 1. F7 F dim F 2. Cm F7 B♭
West Vir-gin-ia, Wis-con-sin, Wy-o-ming. Al-a-o-ming.
Tempo I
F Am Dm C C dim 3 C C dim
North, south, east, west, in our calm, ob-jec-tive o-pin-ion, (name of
C C dim C F Dm
home state) is the best of the Fif-ty nif-ty
B♭ C7 F Dm G7 C7
U-nit-ed States from thir-teen o-rig-i-nal col-o-nies,
F F7 Gm G dim F Am
Shout 'em, scout 'em, Tell all a-bout 'em, One by one till we've
Dm G7 B♭
giv-en a day to ev'-ry state in the good old
D♭ E♭ F
U. S. A.

"The Star-Spangled Banner" was inspired by a battle in the War of 1812. Francis Scott Key, aboard a ship, waited for the outcome of the attack. The "red glare" of artillery fire lit the sky, reassuring him that the American flag still flew. The bombing stopped at dawn. The star-spangled banner still waved. The artist, J. Bower, showed the battle in his etching on page 291.

THE STAR-SPANGLED BANNER

Music Attributed to J. S. Smith
Words by Francis Scott Key

1. Oh, ___ say! can you see, by the dawn's ear - ly light,
2. On the shore, dim - ly seen through the mists of the deep,
3. Oh, ___ thus be it ev-er when ___ free men shall stand

What so proud - ly we hailed at the twi- light's last gleam - ing?
Where the foe's haugh - ty host in dread si - lence re - pos - es,
Be - tween their loved homes and the war's des - o - la - tion!

Whose broad stripes and bright stars, through the per - il - ous fight,
What is that which the breeze, o'er the tow - er - ing steep,
Blest with vic - t'ry and peace, may the heav'n res - cued land

O'er the ram - parts we watched were so gal - lant - ly stream - ing?
As it fit - ful - ly blows, half con - ceals, half dis - clos - es?
Praise the Pow'r that hath made and pre - served us a na - tion.

And the rock - ets' red glare, the bombs burst - ing in air,
Now it catch - es the gleam of the morn - ing's first beam,
Then ___ con - quer we must, for our cause it is just,

| Bb | F | Bb | F | F7 | Bb | Gm | C7 | F |

Gave proof through the night that our flag was still there.
In full glo-ry re-flect-ed now — shines on the stream;
And this be our mot-to, "In— God is our trust."

| F7 | Bb | Eb | G7 | Cm | C7 | Bb | F |

Oh, say, does that — Star-Span-gled Ban-ner — yet — wave —
'Tis the Star-Span-gled — Ban-ner, oh, long may— it — wave —
And the Star-Span-gled — Ban-ner in tri-umph —shall — wave —

| F | F7 | Bb | F | Bb | Gm | C7 | Bb | F7 | Bb |

O'er the land —— of the free and the home of the brave?
O'er the land —— of the free and the home of the brave!
O'er the land —— of the free and the home of the brave!

LISTENING

Washington Post March *by John Philip Sousa*

John Philip Sousa was a famous bandmaster and composer. Because he composed so many marches, he earned the title "The March King." This is one of his most popular marches.

The Bombardment of Fort McHenry, J. Bower, 1814.

Halloween's I Scream

Halloween Montage

LISTENING

Do you recognize these tunes? They all have something to do with the Halloween spirit—identify them if you can!

Halloween is a time when "the shivers" can be fun. Watch for a slight case of these as you sing this old English folk song.

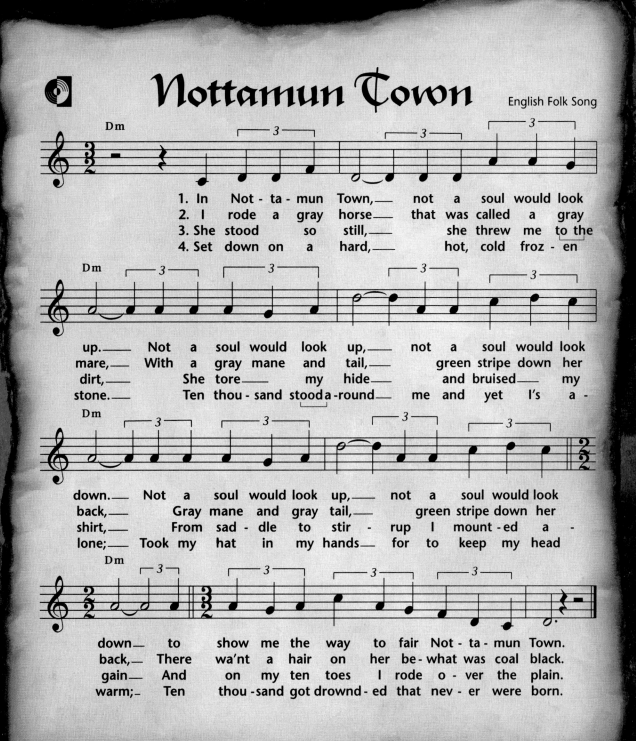

Nottamun Town

English Folk Song

1. In Not - ta - mun Town,— not a soul would look
2. I rode a gray horse— that was called a gray
3. She stood so still,— she threw me to the
4. Set down on a hard,— hot, cold froz - en

up.— Not a soul would look up,— not a soul would look
mare,— With a gray mane and tail,— green stripe down her
dirt,— She tore— my hide— and bruised— my
stone.— Ten thou - sand stood a -round— me and yet I's a -

down.— Not a soul would look up,— not a soul would look
back,— Gray mane and gray tail,— green stripe down her
shirt,— From sad - dle to stir - rup I mount - ed a -
lone;— Took my hat in my hands— for to keep my head

down— to show me the way to fair Not - ta - mun Town.
back,— There wa'nt a hair on her be - what was coal black.
gain— And on my ten toes I rode o - ver the plain.
warm;— Ten thou -sand got drownd - ed that nev - er were born.

from ## The Headless Horseman

The headless horseman rides tonight
through stark and starless skies.
Shattering the silence
with his otherworldly cries,
he races through the darkness
on his alabaster steed.
The headless horseman rides tonight
wherever the fates would lead.

And he rides upon the wind tonight,
he rides upon the wind,
galloping, galloping, galloping on
out of the great oblivion,
galloping till the night is gone,
he rides upon the wind tonight,
he rides upon the wind.

—Jack Prelutsky

Think about the poem "The Headless Horseman" as you sing this song. How does the horseman in this song compare with the one in the poem?

The Horseman

Music by Marilyn Davidson
Words by Walter de la Mare

I heard a horse-man Ride o-ver the hill;

The moon shone clear, The night was still;

His helm was sil-ver, and pale was

he; And the horse he rode was of i-vor-y.

GATHERING FOR Thanksgiving

The early settlers of New England came together to give thanks for a successful corn harvest. We remember this first Pilgrim harvest as we celebrate Thanksgiving today.

Come, Ye Thankful People, Come

Music by Sir George Job Elvey
Words by Henry Alford

1. Come, ye thank-ful peo-ple, come, Raise the song of har-vest home;
2. All the world is God's own field, Fruit un-to his praise to yield;

All is safe-ly gath-ered in Ere the win-ter storms be-gin;
Wheat and tares to-geth-er sown, Un-to joy or sor-row grown;

God, our Mak-er, doth pro-vide For our wants to be sup-plied;
First the blade, and then the ear, Then the full corn shall ap-pear;

Come to God's own tem-ple, come, Raise the song of har-vest home.
Lord of har-vest, grant that we Whole-some grain and pure may be.

For Thy Gracious Blessings

Traditional Melody
Arranged
by Marilyn C. Davidson
Words by Lester S. Bucher

Celebrate the Moon

The people of China, Vietnam, and Thailand, as well as other Southeast Asian countries, celebrate the beauty of the full moon with festivals. Asian American communities in the United States celebrate these holidays with special music, food, and traditions.

The Vietnamese Children's Festival is part of their Mid-Autumn Festival. Dancing and singing children fill the streets, carrying lighted lanterns.

This Vietnamese song honors the full moon.

Tết Trung
Children's Festival

Vietnamese Song
Collected and Transcribed by
Kathy B. Sorensen
English Words by MMH

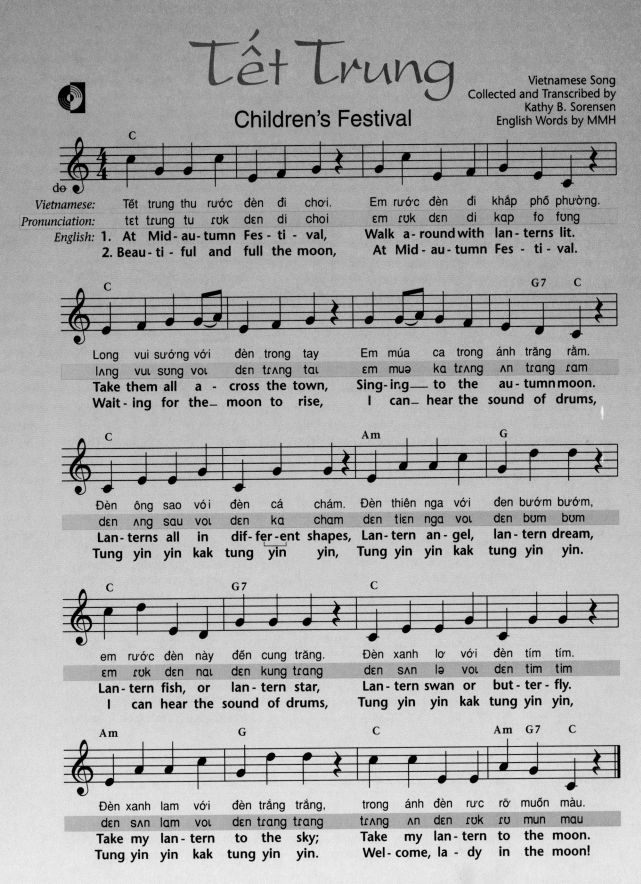

Vietnamese: Tết trung thu rước đèn đi chơi. Em rước đèn đi khắp phố phường.
Pronunciation: tɛt tɾung tu ɾʊk dɛn di choi em ɾʊk dɛn di kap fo fʊng
English: 1. At Mid-au-tumn Fes-ti-val, Walk a-round with lan-terns lit.
2. Beau-ti-ful and full the moon, At Mid-au-tumn Fes-ti-val.

Long vui sướng với đèn trong tay Em múa ca trong ánh trăng rằm.
lʌng vuɪ sʊng voɪ dɛn tɾʌng taɪ em muə ka tɾʌng ʌn tɾang ɾam
Take them all a-cross the town, Sing-ing to the au-tumn moon.
Wait-ing for the moon to rise, I can hear the sound of drums,

Đèn ông sao với đèn cá chám. Đèn thiên nga với đèn bướm bướm,
dɛn ʌng sau voɪ dɛn ka cham dɛn tiɛn nga voɪ dɛn bʊm bʊm
Lan-terns all in dif-fer-ent shapes, Lan-tern an-gel, lan-tern dream,
Tung yin yin kak tung yin yin, Tung yin yin kak tung yin yin.

em rước đèn này đến cung trăng. Đèn xanh lơ với đèn tím tím.
em ɾʊk dɛn naɪ dɛn kung tɾang dɛn sʌn lə voɪ dɛn tim tim
Lan-tern fish, or lan-tern star, Lan-tern swan or but-ter-fly.
I can hear the sound of drums, Tung yin yin kak tung yin yin,

Đèn xanh lam với đèn trắng trắng, trong ánh đèn rực rỡ muôn màu.
dɛn sʌn lam voɪ dɛn tɾang tɾang tɾang ʌn dɛn ɾʊk ɾʊ mun mau
Take my lan-tern to the sky; Take my lan-tern to the moon.
Tung yin yin kak tung yin yin. Wel-come, la-dy in the moon!

Loy Kratong is an autumn ceremony in Thailand. It is a time to forget, or float away, the bad experiences of the year that is ending and hope that the new year will be happy. "Pung Noy Loy Kratong" is often sung at Loy Kratong ceremonies.

Pung Noy Loy Kratong
Full Moon Float

Thai Folk Song
Collected and Transcribed by
Kathy B. Sorensen
English Words by MMH

Thai: ผึ้ง น้อย ลอย กระ ทง รำ วง กัน แบบ ไทย ไทย
Pronunciation: pʊng nɔi lɔi kra tong ɾam wong kan bæb tɑi tɑi
English: Cel - e - brate Loy Kra- tong, Oh, do the float— dance.

เดือน และ ดาว ลอย เด่น เห็น จันทร์ เพ็ญ แล้ว ชื่น ใจ ลำ
duan læ dau lɔi den hen jan pen læu chʊn jai lam
When the ca- nals are full, moon and stars are float - ing. The

คลอง น้ำ นอง เต็ม เปี่ยม เอ๋ย เรียม จะ ช้า อยู่ ใย น้อง
klɔng nam nɔng tem piem əi ɾiem ja cha yu yai nɔng
full moon_ makes us dance, oi!__ Broth - er, why so slow? Broth - er,

เอ๋ย พี่ เอ๋ย น้อง เอ๋ย พี่ เอ๋ย มา รำ วง
əi pi əi nɔng əi pi əi ma ɾam wong
oi!__ Sis- ter, oi! Come,_ oi!__ Let's dance and cel - e -

กัน วัน ลอย กระ ทง มา รำ วง กัน วัน ลอย กระ ทง
kan wan lɔi kra tong ma ɾam wong kan wan lɔi kra tong
brate the Loy Kra- tong, Oh, dance on full moon Loy Kra- tong.

The Moon on High (excerpts)
Chinese Folk Music

Images of the moon are often suggested by music and visual art forms. Musicians play "The Moon on High" on traditional Chinese instruments. You will hear bowed and plucked strings, wind, and percussion instruments.

LISTEN to this traditional Chinese music. Describe how you think the moon portrayed by the music looks.

Celestial Guests (excerpt)
Chinese Folk Melody

*Bill Douglass, an American musician, plays this traditional melody on a Chinese flute. The word **celestial** describes the sun, the moon, the stars and anything else related to the sky. Celestial also describes anything related to China or the Chinese. Why do you think this music is called "Celestial Guests?"*

Celebrating
Loy Kratong
in Thailand.

Loy Kratong is celebrated when the moon is full, and the water is high in the rivers or canals. People make floats out of flowers and send them down the water.

Winter

SNOW

As though pretending to be blooms
The snowflakes scatter in the winter sky.

—Sei Shonāgon

The beauty of winter can be enchanting despite the harsh effects of a cold climate. What sights and sounds come to your mind when you think of winter? Imagine the winter scene described in this song.

WINTER WONDERLAND

Music by Felix Bernard
Arranged by Marilyn Davidson
Words by Dick Smith

Sleigh bells ring, are you lis - t'nin'? In the lane snow is
way is the blue - bird, Here to stay is a

glis - t'nin' A beau - ti - ful sight,__ We're hap - py to - night__
new bird, He sings a love song,__ As we go a - long__

Walk - in' in a win - ter won - der - land! Gone a - land!

Enchantment

F♯   C♯7   F♯

In the mead - ow we can build a snow - man; (And we'll)

F♯   C♯7   F♯

Then pre - tend that he is Par - son Brown.

A   E7   A7

He'll say, "Are you mar - ried?" We'll say, "No, man!____ But

D   E7   A7

you can do the job when you're in town."____ Lat - er

D   A7

on we'll con - spire____ As we dream by the fire____ To

A   G   A7

face un - a - fraid____ the plans that we made____

E7   A7   D

Walk - in' in a win - ter won - der - land.____

Text within illustration:
MARK MY FOOTSTEPS MY GOOD PAGE

TREAD THOU IN THEM BOLDLY

"Mark my footsteps, my good page, . . .", illustrated by Jessie Marion King, 1919

This song tells the story of King Wenceslas and his page going
out to help a poor man on a cold winter night.

**LISTEN to the dialogue between the king and his page.
Are their voices changed or unchanged?**

GOOD KING Wenceslas

Spring Carol
from *Piae Cantiones* 1582
Words by
Rev. John Mason Neale

1. Good King Wen-ces-las look'd out On the feast of Ste-phen,
2. "Hith-er, page, and stand by me, If thou know'st it, tell-ing,
3. "Bring me food and drink so fine, Bring me pine logs hith-er;
4. "Sire, the night is dark-er now, And the wind blows strong-er;
5. In his mast-er's steps he trod, Where the snow lay dint-ed;

When the snow lay round a-bout, Deep and crisp and e-ven;
Yon-der peas-ant, who is he? Where and what his dwell-ing?"
Thou and I shall see him dine When we bear them thith-er."
Fails my heart, I know not how, I can go no long-er."
Heat was in the ver-y sod Which the saint had print-ed;

Bright-ly shone the moon that night, Though the frost was cru-el,
"Sire, he lives a good league hence, Un-der-neath the moun-tain;
Page and mon-arch forth they went, Forth they went to-geth-er,
"Mark my foot-steps, my good page, Tread thou in them bold-ly:
There-fore, ev'-ry-one, be sure, Wealth or rank pos-sess-ing,

When a poor man came in sight, Gath-'ring win-ter fu-el.
Right a-gainst the for-est fence, By Saint Ag-nes' foun-tain."
Through the rude wind's wild la-ment And the bit-ter weath-er.
Thou shalt find the win-ter's rage Freeze thy blood less cold-ly."
Ye who now will bless the poor, Shall your-selves find bless-ing.

THE Festival OF LIGHTS

The ceremony of lighting candles is often part of celebrations. Hanukkah is sometimes called the Festival of Lights.

Hanukkah celebrates an event that took place over 2,000 years ago. After a long fight for freedom, Judah Maccabee led the Jews to victory. Judah and his people found that their city of Jerusalem, including the holy temple, had been treated disrespectfully. The people wanted to relight the holy lamps in the temple since they were supposed to burn at all times. They found only enough oil for one day. Amazingly the oil lasted for eight days.

The word *Hanukkah* means "rededication" in Hebrew. The holy lamps were lit to rededicate the temple.

Families celebrate Hanukkah by gathering to light candles. Each night of the holiday they light one more candle and observe traditions of the holiday.

WHO CAN RETELL?

Music by M. Ravino
Arranged by
Harry Coopersmith
Translation by B.M. Edidin

EIGHT *Are the* LIGHTS

Eight are the lights
   of Hanukkah
We light for a week
   And a day.
We kindle the lights,
   And bless the Lord,
And sing a song,
   And pray.

Eight are the lights
   of Hanukkah
For justice and mercy
   and love,
For charity, courage
   and honor and peace,
And faith in Heaven
   above.

Eight are the lights
   of Hanukkah
To keep ever bright
   Memories
Of the valiant soul
   And the fighting heart
And the hope of the
   Maccabees!

—Ilo Orleans

In Hebrew songs of praise, there is a tradition of substituting syllables or short words for part of the text. This helps to create a strong rhythmic quality in the songs.

Hanerot Halalu

Words and Music by
Baruch J. Cohon
Arranged by Blanche Chass

ha ne rot ha la lu ha ne rot ha la lu ko desh hem

ha ne rot ha la lu ha ne rot ha la lu ko desh hem ya ba

35 *Part 2 Begin very slowly; increase tempo to end; clap on beat.*

bim bom bim bom bim bom bim bom bim bom bim bom ya ba

1.

bim bom bim bom bim bom bim bom bim bom bim bom

Parts 1 & 2 2.

bim bom ya ba bim bom bim bom bim hei

*Besides singing songs and lighting the menorah,
Hanukkah festivities include playing a dreidel game
and exchanging gifts and gelt. Gelt can be real money or
chocolate in the shape of gold coins.*

THE SCANDINAVIAN CHRISTMAS

Scandinavia is a region of Europe that includes Sweden, Norway, and Denmark. These countries share many Christmas customs. Many Scandinavian traditions are practiced in parts of the United States where Scandinavian immigrants settled.

CHRISTMAS AT SANBORN

Carl Larsson painted this Christmas scene in 1907 at his Swedish home. Two other paintings, or panels, fit with this one to create one large picture called a *triptych*. The other panels show more Christmas festivities.

GOD JUL   *GLEDELIG JUL*

312

SEASON

SWEDEN

The holiday season begins long before Christmas in Swedish communities. Santa Lucia Day is celebrated on December 13. Santa Lucia was an Italian saint from the early Christian era. During the Middle Ages, a Swedish peasant thought he saw her walking on a lake. She was dressed in white, wore a crown of lights, and carried gifts of food.

To honor Santa Lucia, the oldest girl in each family rises before dawn. She dresses in white and puts on a crown of evergreens and lights. After waking her family by singing "Santa Lucia," she serves coffee and freshly baked rolls.

LISTENING

Sankta Lucia *Italian Folk Song*

"Sankta Lucia" was originally an Italian song. It traveled to Sweden with the legend of Santa Lucia. Listen to the song in Swedish.

GLAEDELIG JUL

The Swedish holiday season continues into the new year, including much feasting and fun on Christmas Eve and Christmas.

On Knut's Day, January 13, the Swedes clean up after celebrating the holidays, and Christmas is "swept out" for another year.

Nu är det Jul igen
Yuletide Is Here Again

Swedish Dance Carol

Swedish: Nu är det Jul i - gen, och nu är det Jul i - gen, Och
Pronunciation: nu æɾ dɛt yu li yɛn ɔk nu æɾ dɛt yu li yɛn ɔk
English: Yule - tide is here a - gain, Oh, Yule - tide is here a - gain, The

Ju - len va - ra ska' till Pas - ka.
yu lɛn va ɾa ska tɪl pɔ ska
hol - i - days will last 'til Eas - ter. The

Sa är det Pask i - gen, och so är det Pask i - gen, Och
sɔ æɾ dɛt pɔ ski yɛn ɔk sɔ æɾ dɛt pɔ ski yɛn ɔk
Then it is Eas - ter time, Oh, then it is Eas - ter time, and

Pask - en va - ra ska' till Ju - la.
pɔ skɛn va ɾa skɔ tɪl yu la
Eas - ter time will last 'til Yule - tide.

314 THE SCANDINAVIAN CHRISTMAS SEASON

"Ringing in Christmas" is a Norwegian tradition—at 5:00 P.M. on Christmas Eve, church bells ring. That night, many Scandinavian children believe that an elf brings gifts from Santa. In Norway this elf is called *Julenissen*.

Jeg er så glad hver Julekveld
I Am So Glad on Christmas Eve

Norwegian Carol
English Words by MMH

Norwegian:	Jeg	er	så	glad	hver	ju - le - kveld	For
Pronunciation:	yεy	ær	so	gla	vær	yu lə kvɛl	foɾ
English:	I	am	so	glad	on	Christ - mas Eve,	The

da	blev	Je - sus fodt,	Da	lys - te stjer - nen
da	blɛ	ye sus föt	da	lüs tɛ styær nɛn
night when Christ	was born.	That	night the an - gels came

som	en	sol,	Og	en - gle sang	så sodt.
som	ɪn	sul	o	ɛn glɛ sang	so söt
from	on	high,	And	sang their won - der - ful	song.

DENMARK

Christmas stamps, known as
seals, were first introduced in
Denmark in 1904. A Danish
postal clerk suggested selling
special holiday stamps to raise
money for charity. This tradition has spread around the
world. The money raised by
selling Christmas seals in the
United States helps
pay for medical
research.

Deilig er den himmel blå

Oh, How Beautiful the Sky

Danish Folk Carol
Words by Nicolai F. S. Grundtvig
English Words by Ingebret Dorrum

do

Danish: Dei - lig er den him - mel blå, lyst det er at
Pronunciation: daɪ li ɛʌ dɛn hɪ məl blo lüst di ɛʌ æt
English: 1. Oh, how beau - ti - ful the sky, With the spar - kling
2. In the midst of Christ - mas night, While the stars were

se der - på, hvor de gyld - ne stjer - ner blink - er,
si dɛʌ po vor di gül nʌ stiɛr nʌ blɪŋ kʌ
stars on high, How they glit - ter, bright - ly beam - ing,
shin - ing bright, Of a sud - den, clear and ra - diant,

hvor de smil - er, hvor de vink - er, os fra jor - den
vor di smi lʌ vor di vɪŋ kʌ ʌs fra yo rɛn
How they twin - kle, glad - some beam - ing, As they draw our
One ap - peared and shone re - splen - dent, With the lus - ter

op til sig. Os fra jor - den op til sig.
ʌp tɪl saɪ ʌs fra yo rɛn ʌp tɪl saɪ
hearts to heav'n, As they draw our hearts to heav'n.
of the sun, With the lus - ter of the sun.

Burning the Yule log is an old Scandinavian custom that is still popular today. Cold Christmas seasons in northern countries may have inspired this tradition. Long ago, fire was a symbol of home and safety. Today the Yule log is still burned as a pleasant reminder of the old ways.

CHRISTMAS JOY

One of the joys of the Christmas season is the sound of bells. From sleigh bells to church bells, their music is heard. Many words describe the tone color of bells. *Silver* can mean "a soft, resonant sound." Do you think silver describes ringing bells?

Silver Bells

Words and Music by
Jay Livingston and Ray Evans

1. Cit - y side - walks, bus - y side - walks dressed in hol - i - day style
2. Strings of street lights, ev - en stop-lights blink a bright red and green,

In the air there's a feel - ing of Christ-mas._____
As the shop - pers rush home with their trea -sures._____

Chil-dren laugh - ing, peo-ple pass - ing, meet-ing smile af - ter smile,
Hear the snow crunch, see the kids bunch, this is San - ta's big scene,

And on ev' - ry street cor - ner you hear:_____
And a - bove all this bus - tle you hear:_____

Refrain

Sil - ver bells, _____ (Sil - ver bells,) Sil - ver bells, _____ (Sil - ver bells,)

It's Christ - mas time in the cit - y. _____

Ring - a - ling, _____ (Ring - a - ling,) Hear them ring, _____ (Hear them ring,)

Soon it will be Christ - mas day. _____

from

The Bells

Hear the sledges with the bells—
Silver bells!
What a world of merriment their melody foretells!
How they tinkle, tinkle, tinkle,
In the icy air of night!
While the stars, that oversprinkle
All the heavens, seem to twinkle
With a crystalline delight
Keeping time, time, time,
In a sort of Runic rhyme,
To the tintinnabulation that so musically wells
From the bells, bells, bells, bells,
Bells, bells, bells—
From the jingling and the tinkling of the bells.

—Edgar Allan Poe

Most musical traditions on the island of Puerto Rico are Spanish in origin. José Feliciano, who composed "Feliz Navidad," was born in Puerto Rico. He uses both English and Spanish words for Christmas wishes in this song.

Feliz Navidad

Words and Music
by José Feliciano

Spanish: Feliz Navidad. Feliz Navidad, Feliz Navidad, Prospero año y felicidad.

Pronunciation: fe lis nɑ βi ðɑð fe lis nɑ βi ðɑð fe lis nɑ βi ðɑð pros pe ɾo ɑ nyo i fe li si ðɑð

I want to wish you a Merry Christmas
With lots of presents to make you happy.

José Feliciano has won numerous Grammy Awards. He continues to compose and record while performing all over the world.

I want to wish you a Mer - ry Christ - mas from the

bot - tom of my heart.

I want to wish you a Mer - ry Christ - mas with mis - tle - toe and

lots of cheer. With lots of laugh - ter through -

out the years from the bot - tom of my heart.

The words of this Puerto Rican Christmas song describe Mary and Joseph's trip to Bethlehem.

ALEGRÍA, ALEGRÍA
Joy, Joy

Puerto Rican Folk Song
English Version by MMH

Spanish: Ha - cia Be - lén se en - ca - mi - na Ma - ria
Pronunciation: a sya βe len seng ka mi na ma rya
English: On to Be - lén goes Ma - ri - a, lov - ing

con su a - man - te es - po - so lle - van - do en su com - pa -
kon swa man tes po so ye βan doen su kam pa
hus - band close be - side her. God is with them, a com -

ñi - a a to - do un Dios po - de - ro - so. A - le -
nyi a a to doun dyos po de ro so a le
pan - ion, to pro - tect them on their jour - ney. A - le -

grí - a A - le - grí - a A - le - grí - a, A - le - grí - a A - le - grí - a y pla -
gri a le gri a le gri a a le gri a le gri ai pla
grí - a A - le - grí - a A - le - grí - a, A - le - gría, joy and pleas - ure to -

cer que la Vir - gen va de pa - so con su es -
ser ke la βir xen ba ðe pa so kon swes
day. On to Be - lén, they will jour - ney, they will

1. po - so ha - cia Be - lén. A - le -
po soa sya βe len a le
pass us on their way. A - le -

2. po - so ha - cia Be - lén.
po soa sya βe len
pass us on their way.

This song, with its calypso style, expresses the excitement of preparing for Christmas.

MAMA, BAKE THE JOHNNYCAKE, CHRISTMAS COMIN'

Words and Music by
Blake Alphonso Higgs

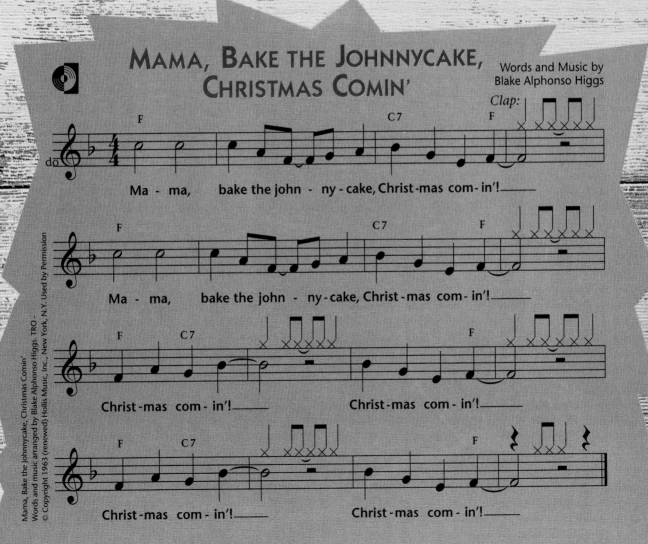

Mama, bake the john - ny - cake, Christ - mas com - in'!

Mama, bake the john - ny - cake, Christ - mas com - in'!

Christ - mas com - in'! Christ - mas com - in'!

Christ - mas com - in'! Christ - mas com - in'!

KWANZAA

Kwanzaa is a holiday observed by many African Americans. Dr. Maulana Karenga created it in 1966. He based Kwanzaa on African harvest celebrations. Families and communities choose their favorite African or African American music to help celebrate. This song, often called the African American National Anthem, is frequently sung during Kwanzaa.

Lift Every Voice and Sing

Music by Rosamond Johnson
Words by James Weldon Johnson

Lift ev'-ry voice and sing, till earth and heav-en ring,

Ring with the har-mo - nies of lib - er - ty.

Let our re-joic-ing rise high as the list-'ning___ skies,

Let it re-sound loud as the roll - ing sea.

Sing a song full of the faith that the dark past has taught us;

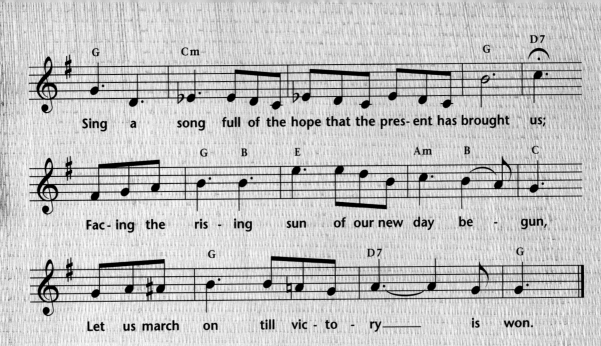

Sing a song full of the hope that the pres- ent has brought us;

Fac- ing the ris - ing sun of our new day be - gun,

Let us march on till vic- to - ry⎯ is won.

Kwanza means "first" in Swahili, a language used in parts of Africa. The holiday name is spelled with an extra *a* to give it seven letters. The number *seven* holds special meaning because of the seven principles of Kwanzaa. The celebration lasts seven days from December 26 to January 1.

Each evening, families light a candle in a candleholder called the *kinara* and discuss one of the seven principles. On the last day of the holiday, the community gathers for a feast with music and dancing called the *karamu.*

LISTENING

Ajaja *by Babatunde Olatunji*

Kwanzaa is a time for all music of African origins. "Ajaja," a modern work, is based on traditional west African music. You will hear many percussion instruments, including several types of drums, agogo bells, and beaded gourds called shekeres.

GREETING THE NEW YEAR

An unknown poet wrote the words to "A New Year Carol." The phrase *levy dew* may come from Welsh words. In modern language, *levy* refers to drawing up water, as in pulling water from a well. *Dew* means "moisture," like the drops of water found on grass in the morning. There was an early British belief that drops of dew gathered on Christmas or May Day had special qualities.

A New Year Carol

Music by Benjamin Britten
Words Anonymous

1. Here we bring new wa - ter from the well____ so clear,
2. Sing____ reign of Fair__ Maid, with____ gold up - on her toe,
3. Sing____ reign of Fair__ Maid, with____ gold up - on her chin,

For to wor - ship God with this hap - py New Year.
O - pen you the West Door and turn the Old Year go.
O - pen you the East Door and let the New Year in.

1., 2.

mf

Sing le - vy dew, sing le - vy dew, the wa - ter and the wine;

The sev - en bright gold wires and the bu - gles that do shine.

3.

pp

Sing le - vy dew, sing le - vy dew, the wa - ter and the wine;

dim. *pp*

The sev - en bright gold wires and the bu - gles that do shine.

Spotlight on

BENJAMIN BRITTEN

Benjamin Britten (1913–1976) was a famous British composer. Growing up, he frustrated his brother and sisters because he monopolized the piano when they wanted to play. Besides writing songs, operas, and symphonies, he also wrote background music for movies. He is well known for his music for children, including The Young Person's Guide to the Orchestra, *which he composed in 1945.*

Let FREEDOM Ring

Dr. Martin Luther King, Jr., devoted his life to achieving freedom and justice for African Americans and people everywhere. The words of this song tell of Dr. King's life and the ideals for which he worked.

The Dream of Martin Luther King

Words and Music by
Merle Gartrell and
Students of Cummings
Elementary School

Allegro

do

1. Once there was a gen-tle-man_____ who talked a-bout a prom-ised land.
2. In his dream he saw the peo-ple of this land__ walk-ing side by side.

_____ He reached out and took the trou-bles of the
_____ White man, black man, red man, yel-low man__

peo-ple in his strong__ black hands.____ He had a dream that
lov-ing one an-oth-er with pride.____ Now he's__ gone a-

ev'-ry-bod-y ought to hear the bells of free-dom ring._____
way be-fore__ the day his dream be-came a real__ thing._____

Now the peo-ple shout and sing a-bout the dream of Mar-tin Lu-ther King.
But he'll hear the an-gels sing a-bout the dream of Mar-tin Lu-ther King.

328

Celebrations Martin Luther King, Jr., Day **329**

The term *civil rights* describes the right of all people to fair treatment. In the 1960s, many people felt it was time to stand up for the civil rights of African Americans.

LISTENING

I Have a Dream (excerpts)

by Dr. Martin Luther King, Jr.

You will hear parts of Dr. King's speech twice—once as delivered by Dr. King, and once read by someone else. Dr. King was a powerful speaker. He spoke to further the cause of civil rights for African Americans, and for all people unfairly treated.

COMPARE the two versions of Dr. King's speech. How are they different?

The words *free at last* have special meaning for African American people. Dr. King used these words in his "I Have a Dream" speech. They have come to represent the hope of all Americans for freedom from the effects of prejudice.

FREE AT LAST

African American Spiritual

All
Dm ... Gm7

Free at last,____ free at last,____

Dm ... A7 Dm *Fine*

Thank God a'-might-y I'm free at last.____

Leader
Dm ... Gm7

1. Sure - ly been 'buked,___ and sure - ly been scorned,____
2. If you don't know___ that I been___ re - deemed,____

Group
Dm ... A7 Dm

Thank God a'-might-y I'm free at last.____

Leader Dm ... Gm7

But still my soul___ is a - heav - en born,____
Just fol - low me___ down to Jor - dan's stream,____

Group
Dm ... A7 Dm *D.C. al Fine*

Thank God a'-might-y I'm free at last.____

THE LUCK OF THE IRISH

"Harrigan" was first performed as part of a play in 1908. George M. Cohan wrote the song during a time in history when great numbers of immigrants were arriving in the United States. Many of these immigrants were Irish.

HARRIGAN

Words and Music by
George M. Cohan

1. Who is the man who will spend or will e - ven lend? Har - ri - gan, that's me! Who is your friend, when you find that you need a friend? Har - ri - gan, that's me!— For I'm just as proud of my name, you see, As an Em - per - or, Czar, or a King could be. Who is the man helps a man ev' - ry - time he can?

2. Who is the man nev - er stood for a 'gad - a - bout'? Har - ri - gan, that's me! Who is the man that the town's simp - ly mad a - bout? Har - ri - gan, that's me!— Thy la - dies and ba - bies are fond of me, I'm— fond of them, too, in re - turn, you see. Who is the gent that's de - serv - ing a mon - u - ment?

All
mf

Har - ri - gan,   that's   me!
Har - ri - gan,   that's   me!

Refrain

H - A - dou-ble- R - I - G - A - N spells Har - ri - gan.

Proud of all the I - rish blood that's in me.
                                             (him).

Nev - er a man can say a word a - gin' me.   H - A -
                                (him).

dou-ble- R - I - G - A - N, you see, —— Is a name that a shame ne - ver

has been con - nect - ed with, Har - ri - gan,   that's   me!

HELP THIS
PLANET EARTH

This photograph by Ansel Adams is a vivid reminder of the beauty of our environment. Such fragile beauty deserves our attention and respect. Imagine this same photograph filled with garbage and covered by a haze of air pollution. These are just two of the problems that confront us and require each of us to take action.

Earth Day is more than 20 years old. Concerns about protecting the planet and preserving natural resources increase daily. Many people celebrate Earth Day by singing songs about the beautiful, but fragile, environment.

DISCUSS how you can help inform people by singing songs about our environment.

The earth revolves on its axis once every 24 hours. The continuous melody of a round is like the continuous motion of our spinning planet.

ROUND THE EARTH TURNS

Music by Mary Goetze
Words by Doug Goodkin

1. Round the earth turns from morn-ing to night.

2. Turn-ing a-gain from dark to the light.

3. Turn-ing and turn-ing for all our de-light.

Meet Raffi

Do you remember Raffi's songs from when you were younger? For many years, Raffi has been a well-loved composer and performer of music for children. More recently, Raffi has turned his attention toward helping to save the environment. Many of his songs celebrate the beauty and wonder of our planet.

LISTEN as Raffi tells about songwriting and how to help save our planet.

Raffi used this photo on his 1990 recording "Evergreen, Everblue."

Evergreen, Everblue

Words and Music by Raffi

Ev-er-green,—— ev - er - blue, As it was in the be-gin-ning,— we've got to see it through.—— Ev - er-green,—— ev - er - blue, At this point in time, it's up to me, it's up to you.——

The rhythms and rhymes of rap music express feelings about life today.

EARTH DAY RAP

Words and Music by
Doug Goodkin

4/4 The sky is high——— and the o-cean is deep, But

we can't treat the plan-et like a gar-bage heap.——— Don't

wreck it, pro-tect it, keep part of it wild,——— And

think a-bout the fu-ture of your great-grand-chi-ld.——— Re-

cy-cle, bi-cy-cle, don't you drive by your-self,——— Don't

buy those plas-tic pro-ducts on the su-per-mar-ket shelf.

Boy-cott, pe-ti-tion, let the big bus-'ness know,——— That if we mess it up here, there's no - where else we can go.

Don't shrug your shoul - ders, say, "What can I do?" On - ly

one per - son can do it and that per - son is you!

Lullaby from the Great Mother Whale to the Baby Seal Pups *by Paul Winter*

Paul Winter's music combines instrumental jazz with recordings of animal voices. He is strongly committed to saving the environment. The out-of-doors inspires much of his music.

Several years ago, Winter had a unique experience. A baby sea lion came ashore and spent the night near his campfire. This piece honors the sea lion pup he and his friends called Silkie.

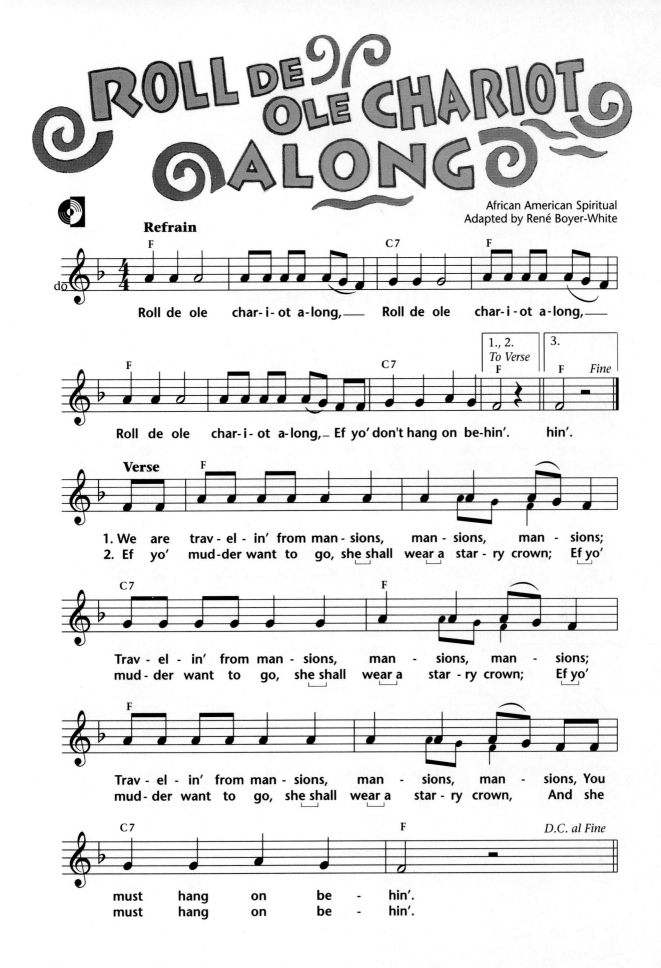

ROLL DE OLE CHARIOT ALONG

African American Spiritual
Adapted by René Boyer-White

Refrain

F

C7

F

Roll de ole char-i-ot a-long,— Roll de ole char-i-ot a-long,—

F

C7

1., 2.
To Verse
F

3.
F *Fine*

Roll de ole char-i-ot a-long,— Ef yo' don't hang on be-hin'. hin'.

Verse

F

1. We are trav-el-in' from man-sions, man-sions, man-sions;
2. Ef yo' mud-der want to go, she shall wear a star-ry crown; Ef yo'

C7

F

Trav-el-in' from man-sions, man-sions, man-sions;
mud-der want to go, she shall wear a star-ry crown; Ef yo'

F

Trav-el-in' from man-sions, man-sions, man-sions, You
mud-der want to go, she shall wear a star-ry crown, And she

C7

F

D.C. al Fine

must hang on be-hin'.
must hang on be-hin'.

Hong Tsai Me Me

Rainbow Sister

Chinese Folk Song
Collected and Transcribed by Kathy B. Sorensen
English Words by MMH

Mandarin: 紅 彩 妹 妹 嗯 嗳 哎 喲
Pronunciation: hɔng tsai me me ʌn ai ei yo
English: 1. Rain - bow___ sis - ter,___ kind___ and good.
2. In the___ spring, with___ flow - ers bright.

長 得 那 麼 嗯 嗳 哎 喲
jang də na mɔ ʌn ai ei yo
I would___ see her___ if___ I could.
I met___ sis - ter___ there___ one night.

櫻 桃 小 嘴 嗯 哎 呦 喲
ing tau shiau jwe ʌn ai ei yo
I can't for - get___ her,___ I don't know why,___
In the___ fall,___ when___ flow - ers die,

一 點 點 那 麼 嗯 哎 呦 喲
i dien dien na mɔ ʌn ai ei yo
Think - ing of her,___ I al - ways cry.
Rain - bow sis - ter___ said___ good - bye.

Verse

American Song

Leader
1. There's a gal in Bal - ti - more,
2. Come, my love, and mar - ry me,
3. If you'll come and be my own,
4. We'll have chick - ens 'round our door,

Group
Li'l 'Li - za Jane,

Leader
She's the one that I a - dore,
I will take good care of thee,
We'll eat ham and sweet corn pone,
Brus - sels car - pet on our floor,

Group
Li'l 'Li - za Jane.

Refrain

All
O E - li - za, Li'l 'Li - za Jane,

O E - li - za, Li'l 'Li - za Jane.

TRAMPIN'

African American Spiritual
Adapted by René Boyer-White

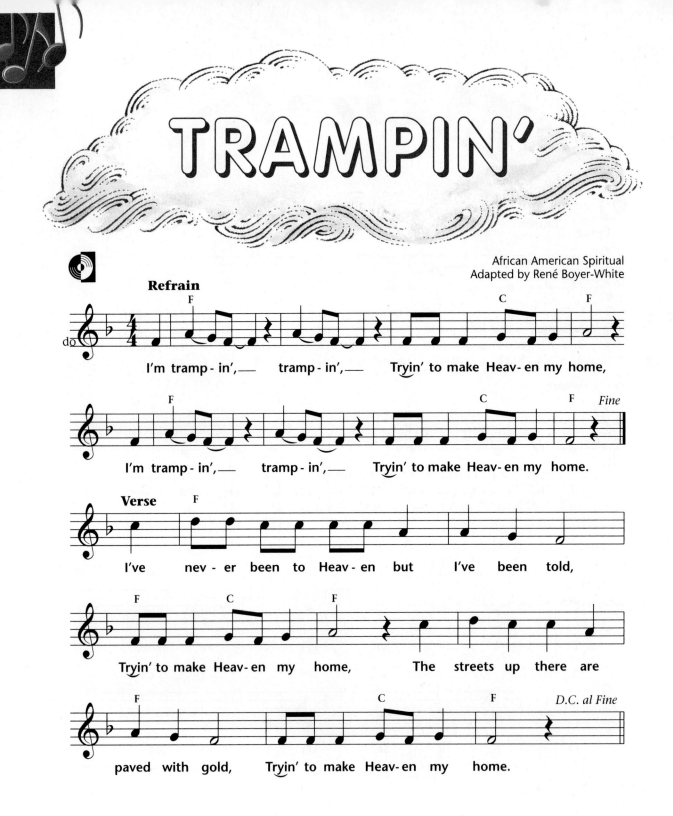

Refrain

I'm tramp-in',— tramp-in',— Tryin' to make Heav-en my home,

I'm tramp-in',— tramp-in',— Tryin' to make Heav-en my home. *Fine*

Verse

I've nev-er been to Heav-en but I've been told,

Tryin' to make Heav-en my home, The streets up there are

D.C. al Fine

paved with gold, Tryin' to make Heav-en my home.

NINE HUNDRED MILES

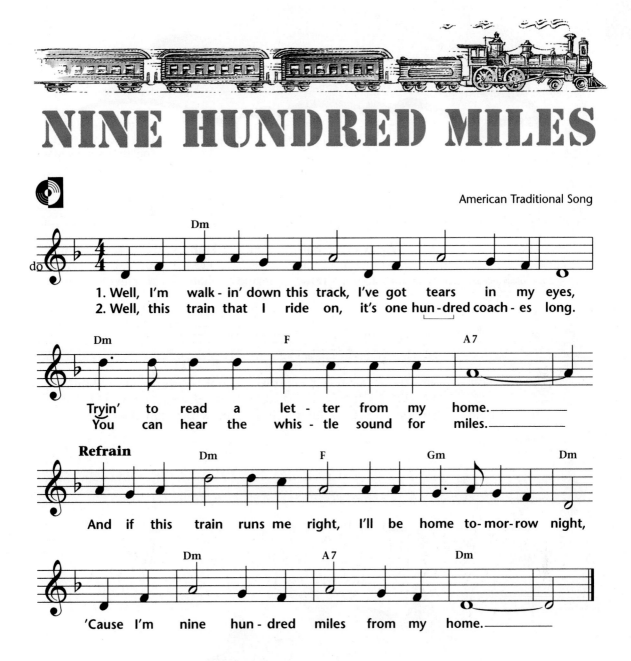

American Traditional Song

1. Well, I'm walk-in' down this track, I've got tears in my eyes,
2. Well, this train that I ride on, it's one hun-dred coach-es long.

Tryin' to read a let-ter from my home.____
You can hear the whis-tle sound for miles.____

Refrain

And if this train runs me right, I'll be home to-mor-row night,

'Cause I'm nine hun-dred miles from my home.____

Wachet auf
Waken Now

Words and Music by
Johann Jakob Wachsmann
English Words by MMH

German: Wach - et auf, Wach-et auf es kräh - te der Hahn,
Pronunciation: va xət aʊf va xət aʊf ɛs kre tə deɾ han
English: Wak - en now, Wak- en now, proud chan - ti - cleer cries,

die Son - ne be - tritt ____ die gol - de - ne Bahn.
di zɔ nə bə trɪt di gɔl də nə ban
The gold - en sun fol - lows its path through the skies.

Ostinato

Wach - et auf, Wach - et auf.
va xət aʊf va xət aʊf
Wak - en now, Wak - en now.

STAR CANON

Music by Mary Goetze
Words from *Firefly* by Li Po

I think, ____ if you flew up to the sky be -

side— the— moon,— you would spar - kle like a star, ____ Oh, ____

MI GALLO
MY ROOSTER

Three-part round
English Words by MMH

1

Spanish: Mi ga-llo se mu-rió a-yer,
Pronunciation: mi ga yo se mu ɾyo a yeɾ
English: My roost-er just died yes-ter-day,

Mi ga-llo se mu-rió a-yer.
mi ga yo se mu ɾyo a yeɾ
My roost-er just died yes-ter-day.

2

Ya no can-ta-rá co-co-rí, co-co-rá,
ya no can ta ɾa ko ko ɾi ko ko ɾa
He will nev-er sing co-co-rí, co-co-rá,

Ya no can-ta-rá co-co-rí, co-co-rá.
ya no can ta ɾa ko ko ɾi ko ko ɾa
He will nev-er sing co-co-rí, co-co-rá.

3

Co-co-rí, co-rí, co-rá,_____
ko ko ɾi ko ɾi ko ɾa
Co-co-rí, co-rí, co-rá,_____

Co-co-rí, co-rí, co-rá._____
ko ko ɾi ko ɾi ko ɾa
Co-co-rí, co-rí, co-rá._____

Der Frühling
THE SPRING

German Round
English Words by MMH

1
F   C7   F

German: Es tö - nen die Lie - der, der Früh - ling kehrt wie - der,
Pronunciation: ɛs tö nən di li dər der frü lıng keɾt vi dər
English: The glad songs are ring - ing, for spring is re - turn - ing,

2
F   C7   F

Es spie - let— der— Hir - te auf sei - ner— Schal - mei.
ɛs shpi lət der hiɾ tə ɑuf sɑı nəɾ shal mɑı
The shep- herd— is— play - ing up - on his— schal - mei.

3
F   C7   F

La la - la la - la la - la la, la, la, la - la la - la la - la la!

Music by Benjamin Britten
Words by Walter de la Mare

THE THING

Moderately bright

Words and Music by Charles R. Grean

C

do

1. While I was walk - ing down the beach one
2. I picked it up and ran to town as
3. I turned a - round and got right out a -
4. I wan - dered all a - round the town un -
5. I wan - dered on for man - y years, a

F   **C**   **G7**   **C**

bright and sun - ny day,_____ I saw a great big
hap - py as a king._____ I took it to a
run - nin' for my life,_____ And then I took it
til I chanced to meet_____ a ho - bo who was
vic - tim of my fate._____ Un - til one day I

C   **D7**

wood - en box a - float - in' in the
guy I know who'd buy most an - y -
home with me to give it to my
look - ing for a hand - out on the
came up - on Saint Pe - ter at the

G7   **C**

bay._____ I pulled it in and
thing._____ But this is what he
wife._____ But this is what she
street._____ He said he'd take most
gate._____ And when I tried to

THE THING. Words and Music by Charles R. Grean. TRO - © Copyright 1950 (renewed) Hollis Music, Inc., New York, NY. Used by Permission. © Grean Music Co.

6. The moral of the story is if you're out on the beach
   And you should see a great big box and it's within your reach,
   Don't ever stop and open it up, that's my advice to you,
   'cause you'll never get rid of the xxx, no matter what you do.
   Oh, you'll never get rid of the xxx, no matter what you do.

By the Singing Water

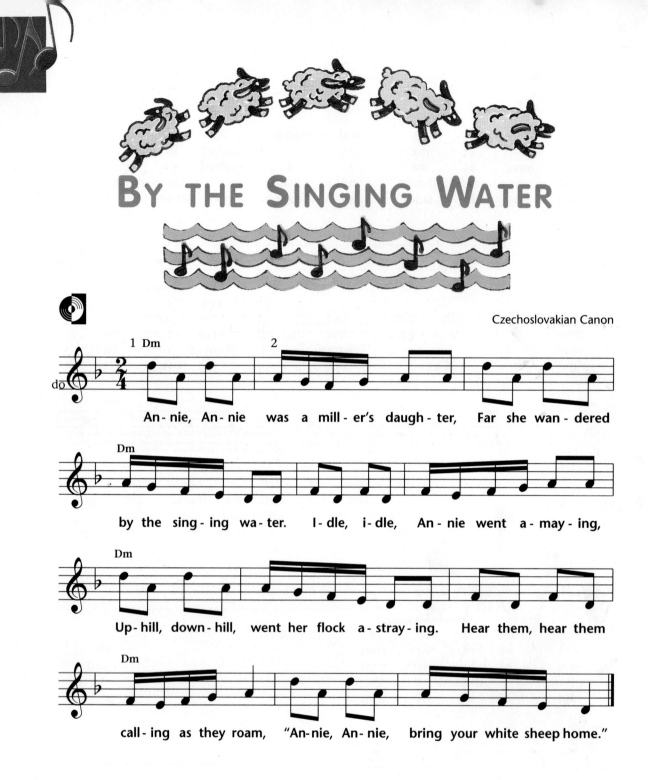

Czechoslovakian Canon

An-nie, An-nie was a mill-er's daugh-ter, Far she wan-dered

by the sing-ing wa-ter. I-dle, i-dle, An-nie went a-may-ing,

Up-hill, down-hill, went her flock a-stray-ing. Hear them, hear them

call-ing as they roam, "An-nie, An-nie, bring your white sheep home."

DON MARTÍN

Mexican Folk Song
English Words by MMH

Spanish: A Don Mar - tín, ti - ri - rin - tin - tin, Se le mu -
Pronunciation: a ðon maɾ tin ti ɾi ɾin tin tin se le mu
English: Oh, Don Mar - tin, ti - ri - rin - tin - tin, His chil - dren

rió, to - ro - ron - ton - ton, Su chi - qui - tin, ti - ri - rin - tin -
ɾyo to ɾo ɾon ton ton su chi ki tin ti ɾi ɾin tin
cried, to - ro - ron - ton - ton, They got the mea - sles, ti - ri - rin - tin -

tin, De sa - ram - pión to - ro - ron - ton - ton.
tin de sa ɾam pyon to ɾo ɾon ton ton
tin, And then they died! to - ro - ron - ton - ton.

Tzena, Tzena

Music by Issachar Miron and Julius Grossman
Words by Mitchell Parish

Hebrew/English: **Tze**- na, tze - na, tze - na, tze - na, Hear the hap - py sounds of dan - cing,
Pronunciation: tsɛ nɑ tsɛ nɑ tsɛ nɑ tsɛ nɑ

Tze - na, tze - na, tze - na, tze - na, Ev' - ry - one can sing a - long, so

come____ and dance a - long.
join____ us in our   song.

La la la la,

la la la la la la,   Join us as we dance to - geth - er, sing - ing.

La la la la,   la la la la la la,   Join us in our hap - py

song.   Clap your hands and   *(clap)* raise your voic - es high - er,

Make a cir - cle   while we dance a - round the fire.___ Dance the ho - ra

(clap) to your heart's de - sire.___ All the world sings Tze - na, tze - na, tze - na.

En la feria de San Juan

Puerto Rican Folk Song
Arranged by MMH

All (Groups 1-4)

G   D7

Spanish: 1. En la fe - ria de San Juan, yo com - pré un pi -
Pronunciation: en la fe ɾya ðe san xwan yo kom pɾe un pi

G   *Group 1 only*   D7   G

tí - o, pi - ti, pi - ti, pi - ti, el pi - tí - o.
ti o pi ti pi ti pi ti el pi ti o

(A) *All*

C   G   D7   G

Ven - ga u -sted, ven- ga u - sted, a la fe - ria de San Juan. Ven- ga u-
ßeng gau steð ßeng gau steð a la fe ɾya ðe san xwan ßeng gau

C   G   D7   C   D7   *1. (to Circle B)*
                                        G

sted, ven- ga u - sted, a la fe - ria de San Juan.
steð ßeng gau steð a la fe ɾya ðe san xwan

2. (to Circle C)   *4. (to Coda)*
3. (to Circle D)   G   (B) *All*   G
3

Juan.   2. En la fe - ria de San
xwan   en la fe ɾya ðe san

Group 2 only
D7   G   D7

Juan, yo com - pré un tam - bor, ton, ton, ton, el tam -
xwan yo kom pɾe un tam boɾ ton ton ton el tam

Music Library *Reading Anthology* **355**

KALINKA
Little Snowball Bush

Slowly, gradually faster
Refrain

Russian Folk Song
English Words by MMH

Russian: Ка - лин - ка, ка - лин - ка, ка - лин - ка мо -
Pronunciation: ka lin ka ka lin ka ka lin ka mɔ
English: Ka - lin - ka, ka - lin - ka, ka - lin - ka

я! В са - ду я - го - да ма - лин - ка, ма - лин - ка мо -
ya vsa du ya gɔ da ma lin ka ma lin ka mɔ
mine! In the gar - den grows a ber - ry so sweet and

1. я! Ка - я.
   ya ka
   fine. Ka -

2. Ах,
   ya ax
   fine. Oh,

Verse

Под__ сос - но - ю, под__ зе - лё - но - ю,
pɔd sɔs nɔ yu pɔd zɛ lyo nɔ yu
1. Un - der the__ pine tree, un - der the__ green tree,
2. Stur - dy____ pine tree, shad - y ev - er - green tree,
3. Oh,__ my good__ friend, do not__ for - sake me,

358

Спать по - ло - жи - те_____ вы ме - ня. А -
spat pɔ lɔ ʒi te vɪ mɛ nʲa ɑ
There I'll_____ lay_____ me_____ down to sleep. Ah!
Do not_____ wake me with your rust - ling sound. Ah!
Pro - mise that al - ways you will stand by me! Ah!

Ай_____ лю - ли, лю - ли, ай_____ лю - ли,_____
ɑɪ lyu li lyu li ɑɪ lyu li
Ay,_____ liu - li, liu - li, ay,_____ liu - li,_____

Спать по - ло - жи - те_____ вы ме - ня! Ка -
spat pɔ lɔ ʒi te vɪ mɛ nʲa kɑ
There I'll_____ lay_____ me_____ down to sleep. Ka -
Do not_____ wake me with your rust - ling sound. Ka -
Pro - mise that al - ways you will stand by me! Ka -

To Music

16th-Century German Chorale Melody
Words and Arrangement by Betty Bertaux
Arrangement Adapted by Judy Bond

1. To sing-ing and to mu - sic, to joy - ful friend-ship true;
2. Lift ev' - ry voice to mu - sic, to love's ex - pres-sion sing;
3. For through this gift to hu - man-kind, we each___ to all be - long;

To mo - ments filled with hap - pi - ness, re-fresh-ing each day a - new.
Let mu - sic live in mind and heart, let joy___ and laugh-ter ring!
It's mu - sic that has joined___ us in life's___ sweet mas - ter song.

From___ val - leys and from hill - tops, from sea to shin - ing___ sea,
From___ val - leys and from hill - tops, from sea to shin - ing___ sea,
From the val - leys and from hill - tops, from sea to shin - ing___ sea,

Let earth re-sound with mu - sic, and life___ the rich - er be.

Add harmony on Verse 3

From the val - leys and from hill - tops, from sea to shin - ing___ sea,

Let earth re-sound with mu - sic, and life___ the rich - er___ be.

N'kosi Sikelel' i Afrika

Prayer for Africa

Words and Music by
Enoch Sontonga

Moderate

Zulu: N'ko - si si - ke - lel' i Af - ri - ka, Ma - lu - pha - ka - nyi - sw' u -
Pronunciation: nkɔ si si kɛ lɛ li a fɾi ka ma lu pa ka nyi su
English: Bless, O Lord, our coun-try Af - ri - ca, So that all may see her

phon- do lwa- yo; Yiz- wa im - i - than- da - zo ye- thu.
pɔn dɔ lwa yo yiz wa im i tan da zo yɛ tu
glo- ry held high; Lis- ten and pro- tect us, be our guide.

1.
N'ko - si si - ke - le - la, N'ko - si si - ke - le - la.
nkɔ si si kɛ lɛ la nkɔ si si kɛ lɛ la
Bless our moth- er Af - ri- ca. Bless our moth- er Af - ri- ca.

2.
Thi - na lu - sa - pho lwa- yo. Wo- za mo - ya,_____
ti na lu sa pɔ lwa yo wɔ za mɔ ya
Bless our _____ moth- er Af - ri- ca. Spir- it de- scend,_____

Wo- za mo - ya,_____ Wo- za mo - ya, o - yi - ngcwe - le.
wɔ za mɔ ya wɔ za mɔ ya ɔ ying ʇwɛ lɛ
Spir- it de- scend,_____ Spir- it de- scend, Spir- it de- scend, Spir- it di- vine.

U - si - si- ke- le - la. Thi - na lu - sa - pho lwa- yo.
u si si kɛ lɛ la ti na lu sa pɔ lwa yo
Bless our moth- er Af - ri- ca. Bless our_____ moth- er Af - ri- ca.

THEME FROM

NEW YORK, NEW YORK

Music by John Kander
Words by Fred Ebb

Moderately, with Rhythm

Start spread-in' the news, I'm leav-ing to-day,

I wan-na be a part— of it, New York, New York.

These vag-a-bond shoes are long-ing to stray,

And step a-round the heart— of it, New York, New York.

I wan-na wake up in the cit-y that does-n't sleep

California, Here I Come

Words and Music by B.G. DeSylva,
Al Jolson, and Joseph Meyer

Cal - i - for - nia, here I come,

Right back where I start - ed from.

Where bow - ers of flow - ers bloom in the sun.

Each morn - ing, at dawn - ing, bird - ies sing and ev' - ry - thing.

A sun - kissed miss said, "Don't be late."

That's why I can hard - ly wait.

O - pen up that Gold - en Gate! Cal - i -

for - nia, here I come! come!

Going to Boston

American Play-Party Song

1. Good - bye, girls, I'm goin' to Bos - ton, Good - bye, girls, I'm
2. Clear the way, you'll get run o - ver, Clear the way, you'll
3. Sad - dle up, girls, and we'll go with them, Sad - dle up, girls, and

goin' to Bos - ton, Good - bye, girls, I'm goin' to Bos - ton,
get run o - ver, Clear the way, you'll get run o - ver,
we'll go with them, Sad - dle up, girls, and we'll go with them,

Ear - ly in the morn - ing.

Refrain

Won't we look pret-ty in the ball - room? Won't we look pret-ty in the ball - room?

Won't we look pret-ty in the ball - room? Ear - ly in the morn - ing.

Carolina
in the Morning

Music by Walter Donaldson
Words by Gus Kahn

Liltingly

1. Noth - ing could be fin - er than to be in Car - o - li - na in the
2. Stroll - ing with my girl - ie where the dew is pearl - y ear - ly in the

morn - ing. No one could be sweet - er than my
morn - ing. But - ter - flies all flut - ter up and

sweet - ie, when I meet her in the morn - ing.
kiss each lit - tle but - ter-cup at dawn - ing.

Where the morn - ing glo - ries twine a - round— my door,

Whis - per - ing pret - ty sto - ries I long to hear— once more.

2. If I had A-lad-din's lamp for on-ly a day,— I'd make a wish and here's what I'd say:—— "Noth - ing could be fin - er than to be in Car - o - li - na in the morn - ing."

Mrs. Murphy's Chowder

Words and Music by Oscar Brand

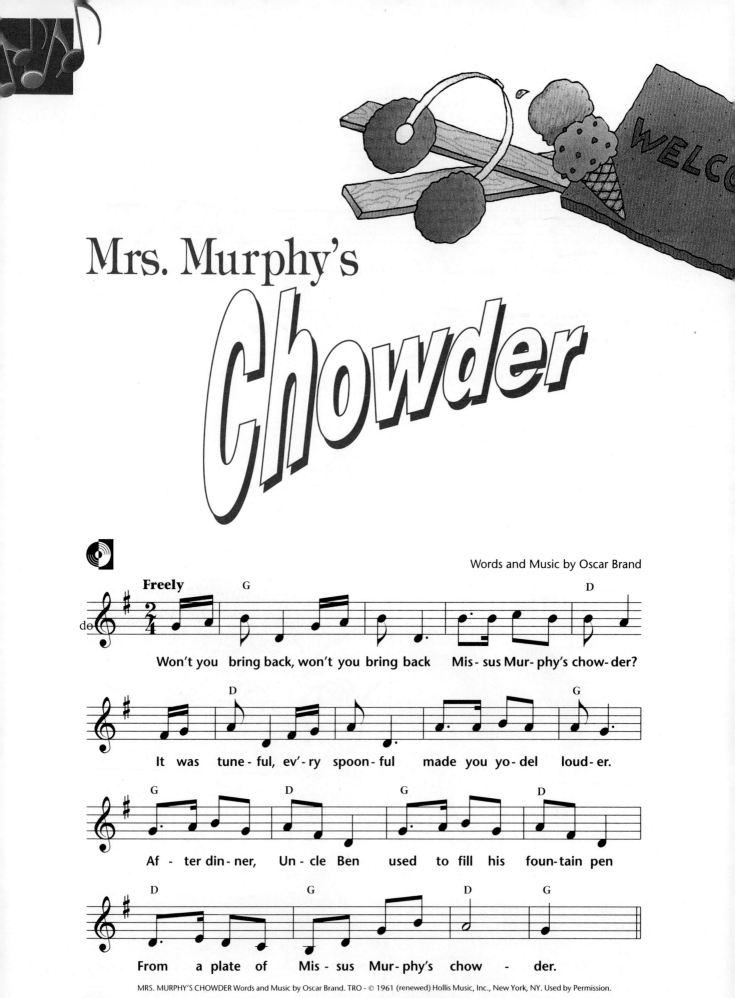

Freely

Won't you bring back, won't you bring back Mis-sus Mur-phy's chow-der?

It was tune-ful, ev'-ry spoon-ful made you yo-del loud-er.

Af - ter din-ner, Un-cle Ben used to fill his foun-tain pen

From a plate of Mis-sus Mur-phy's chow - der.

Refrain

faster

It had { ice cream, cold cream, ben - zine, gas - o - line,
Sponge cake, beef - steak, mis - take, stom - ach - ache,

Soup beans, string beans, float - ing all a - round; Silk hats, door - mats,
Cream puffs, ear - muffs, man - y to be found;

bed slats, Dem - o - crats; Cow - bells, door - bells beck - on you to dine;

Meat - balls, fish balls, moth - balls, can - non - balls. Come on in; the chow - der's fine!

MIDNIGHT

Words and Music by Robert Starer

Gently moving

It is mid-night; it is mid-night. The

sun is shin-ing bright-ly, and a car is rac-ing slow-ly down the ri-ver.

It is sum-mer; it is sum-mer.

Snow is fall-ing light-ly. It is warm and yet I

shiv-er. I saw a rock-et walk.— I heard a tur-tle talk.— I saw a

dog with three legs. I saw four square eggs. Do you know, do you know why I

Singing in chorus is a very exciting and rewarding musical experience. It provides the opportunity for you to join with others in practicing and performing beautiful music and in achieving a high level of artistic excellence.

In this Choral Anthology, you will develop your voice through more challenging music. Each song has warmups to prepare you for singing the song. The songs are written in different languages and represent a variety of styles. Learning to sing these songs expressively, as well as the other choral skills you learn, will prepare you to participate in the joy of choral singing for the rest of your life.

PREPARING FOR SINGING "WIND ON THE HILL"

A. A. Milne has written some of the most beloved poetry and stories for children, including *Winnie-the-Pooh.* Victoria Ebel-Sabo composed this beautiful melody especially for Milne's poem "Wind on the Hill."

DISCOVER the rhyme scheme of the lyrics. Then look at the melody and decide on its form.

LISTEN to the song, following the notation, and notice that the melody moves primarily in a stepwise manner.

SING the pitches in the E minor scale to establish the tonality. Then sing one of the three pitches in the tune-up.

FIND the larger intervals in the song and practice them. Notice that low D is sharped, which makes it D♯.

Wind on the Hill

Music by Victoria Ebel-Sabo
Words by A.A. Milne

No one can tell me, _____ no-bod-y knows _____

_____ Where the wind comes from, _____ where the wind goes, _____

goes, _____ where the wind goes.

It's fly-ing from some-where fast as it can. _____ I could-n't keep

up with it, _____ not if I ran. _____ No one can

PREPARING FOR SINGING "DODI LI"

SING an echo pattern on the word *alleluia* using the "pure" vowels of *ah, eh,* and *oo.* Be sure your jaw is open and relaxed.

Practice the vowel sounds in "Dodi Li" to make them as uniform and accurate as possible. Match your sound with the person next to you.

Dodi Li

Israeli Folk Song
Arranged by Doreen Rao
Transcribed by Nira Chen
Words from Song of
Solomon 2:16, 3:6, 4:9, 4:16

PREPARING FOR SINGING "A TREE TOAD"

"A Tree Toad" is a humorous tongue twister that requires crisp diction for an effective performance.

FIND the dynamics markings in the score: *mp*, *mf*, *p*, *f*, *diminuendo*, and *crescendo*. Then find the articulation markings: stress ♩, staccato ♩, and accent ♩. A *stress* gives a slight emphasis to the note. *Staccato* means the notes are detached or separated. The *accent* makes the note stronger and often louder.

ECHO each phrase of the song with the correct dynamics and articulation. Then establish the tonality of E♭ major by singing up and down the E♭ major scale.

E♭ major scale

do   re   mi   fa   so   la   ti   do'

A Tree Toad

Music by Ruth Watson Henderson
Words Anonymous

A tree— toad loved a   she - toad that— lived— up   in   a   tree.

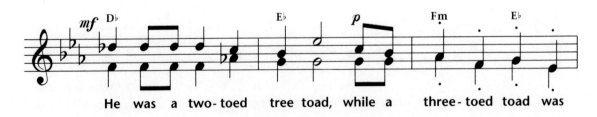

He   was   a two - toed   tree toad, while   a   three - toed toad was

PREPARING FOR SINGING "THE SIDE SHOW"

"The Side Show" was composed by Charles Ives (1874–1954), one of the greatest American composers. Ives was an insurance salesman and did not have to rely on composing to earn a living. Consequently, he had the freedom to please only himself in his music. At times, his melodies take strange turns and the rhythms are unusual.

IDENTIFY the meter signature. Does it remain the same throughout the piece? Which note gets the beat?

PRACTICE the $\frac{3}{4}$ and $\frac{2}{4}$ conducting patterns given below. These will help you feel the change from three beats in a measure to two beats in a measure. How will you conduct the $\frac{5}{4}$ measure?

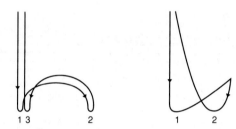

CLAP the following rhythm patterns. Then find them in the song.

SING up the scale and continue up to high *so* to establish the tonality of A♭ major.

A♭ major scale

do re mi fa so la ti do' re' mi' fa' so' fa' mi' re' do'

DISCOVER the places where the music moves in a scale-wise manner. Practice singing those passages. Where does the music change to two parts?

THE SIDE SHOW

Words and Music by
Charles E. Ives

PREPARING FOR SINGING "CHACARERA"

This song is a traditional dance of the Argentine people. The words are in Spanish and tell of the wheat fields and the sounds of the birds.

The rhythm of this song is very important and must be performed accurately. Practice the following two phrases.

DISCOVER how many times each of these phrases is repeated throughout the song.

Notice that the song has four verses plus a short coda. In Verses 1, 3, and 4, the two parts sing the same rhythm. In Verse 2, the two vocal parts sing different rhythms.

FIND the accidentals in the song.

NOTICE that the song changes between major and minor.

CHACARERA
CHATTERBOX

Argentine Folk Song
English Version by MMH

Spanish: 1. Cha - ca - re - ra,— cha - ca - re - ra Me ha can - ta -
Pronunciation: cha ka ɾe ɾa cha ka ɾe ɾa mea kan ta
English: Cha - ca - re - ra,— cha - ca - re - ra A hum - ming -

do un pi - ca - flor. Que con las a - lon - dras
doun pi ka flor ke kon las a lon dɾas
bird— sang— to me: That the larks all— sing— at

380

3. Cha - ca - re - ra,—— cha - ca - re - ra Me ha con - ta-
ʧa ka ɾe ɾa ʧa ka ɾe ɾa mea kon ta
Cha - ca - re - ra,—— cha - ca - re - ra A tur - tle-

do u - na—— tor - caz Que las a - guas— del— a-
ðou na toɾ kas ke las a gwas ðel a
dove— told— me so: That the flow - ing— of— the

rro - yo—— te sal - pi - can— por— ju - gar.
ɾo yo te sol pi kan poɾ xu gaɾ
riv - er,—— will bring wa - ter— to—— the land.

Part 1 ══════════ **f** D

4. Cha - ca - re - ra,—— cha - ca - re - ra Can - ta, can-
ʧa ka ɾe ɾa ʧa ka ɾe ɾa kan ta kan
Cha - ca - re - ra,—— cha - ca - re - ra Sing oh, sing,-

Part 2 ══════════ **f**

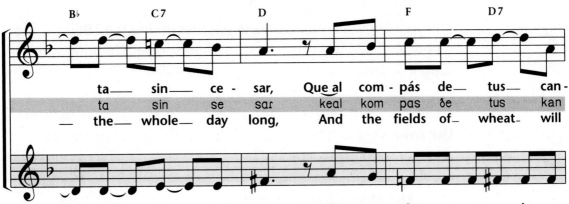

PREPARING FOR SINGING "IF I HAD A HAMMER"

This well-known song was made popular during the 1960s by the American folk singers Lee Hays and Pete Seeger. The song was sung frequently at civil rights and peace rallies.

DISCOVER which parts are singing the melody in each of the four verses. The music in the parts not singing the melody are countermelodies.

CLAP the rhythm of the melody as you say the words.

SING up and down the E♭ major scale and continue down to B♭ to establish the tonality of E♭ major.

do   re   mi   fa   so   la   ti   do'   ti   la   so   fa   mi   re   do   ti,   la,   so,

IF I HAD A HAMMER

Words and Music by
Lee Hays and Pete Seeger
Arranged by Mary Goetze

Parts 1-3: 1. If I had a ham - mer,—— I'd ham-mer in the
(2.) bell,———— I'd ring it in the
(3.) song,———— I'd sing it in the
(4.) ham - mer,—— And I've—— got a

(On Verses 2 and 4) Part 3: **Ring it in the morn.**

(On Verses 3 and 4) Part 2: **Sing ah,————**

If I HAD A HAMMER (The Hammer Song). Words and Music by Lee Hays and Pete Seeger.
TRO - © Copyright 1958 (renewed) 1962 (renewed) Ludlow Music, Inc., New York, NY. Used by Permission.

warn - ing,——— I'd ham - mer out love be - tween my
warn - ing,——— I'd ring—— out love be - tween my
warn - ing,——— I'd sing—— out love be - tween my
free - dom,——— It's a song a - bout love be - tween my

Ding Dong Ding, Love be - tween my

Warn - ing! Warn - ing! Love be - tween my

broth - ers and my sis - ters, All——————————— o - ver this

broth - ers and my sis - ters,

broth - ers and my sis - ters,

Chamber Music Concert

Chamber music is written for a small group of instruments. Only one performer plays on each part. Originally, this music was often played in a chamber, or room, instead of a concert hall, church, or theater. Today, chamber music can be heard on recordings, on the radio or television, or in concert halls. Many instrumentalists enjoy playing chamber music in their homes.

woodwind quintet

brass quintet

When the musicians enter for a concert, clap to greet them. As they perform, listen to the complete piece, then show your appreciation by clapping. If the piece has several movements, clap only at the end of the piece rather than at the end of each movement.

You may notice the musicians nodding or swaying as they play. Since chamber music is played without a conductor, the musicians use these movements to communicate with each other about starting, stopping, or staying together.

LISTENING

Chamber Music Concert
Presented by Smalltown Chamber Players

"RONDEAU" FROM SYMPHONIES .... Jean-Joseph Mouret
DE FANFARES, No. 1

Smalltown Brass Quintet

SUITE FOR WIND QUINTET, ... Ruth Crawford-Seeger
FIRST MOVEMENT

Smalltown Woodwind Quintet

Intermission

STRING QUARTET IN B MINOR, ... Teresa Carreño
FOURTH MOVEMENT

STRING QUARTET OP. 33, No. 3, ... Franz Joseph Haydn
FOURTH MOVEMENT

Smalltown String Quartet

string quartet

PLAN your own chamber music concert. Choose recordings or put together a program that those in your school can play. Prepare the program and present it.

Listening

Composers use many different styles to express their musical ideas. Listen to the variety of sounds in the pieces below.

Gaudeamus omnes
GREGORIAN CHANT
ca. 600-850

Brandenburg Concerto No. 2
Third Movement

JOHANN SEBASTIAN BACH
1721

Trumpet Concerto in E♭
First Movement

FRANZ JOSEPH HAYDN
1796